T0363229

AUSTRALIAN
FISH ID
POCKET GUIDE

First Published 2013
Reprinted 2014, 2015, 2018, 2019, 2020, 2021, 2022. 2023

Published and distributed by
Australian Fishing Network
PO Box 544 Croydon, Victoria 3136
Telephone: (03) 9729 8788
Email: sales@afn.com.au   Website: www.afn.com.au

© Australian Fishing Network 2021

ISBN 9781865132280

Design and production by Australian Fishing Network
Illustrations by Trevor Hawkins

INTRODUCTION

There are many books describing the species that are caught by recreational anglers in Australia. Some of these books are good and some are not so good, but they are either written for scientists or beginners. There is a need for a book which describes fish in language that most anglers can understand and apply in the field or later when they are admiring their prize.

This book provides the information on the species that are regularly taken including their identification and range and some helpful fishing information. This book will be a useful addition to the bookshelves of the keen and occasional recreational fisher in Australia. It is hoped that those who care enough to buy a book of this kind will follow a few simple rules to ensure that future fishing is available. These include:

taking only as many fish as you need, irrespective of the bag limits;
taking ice and ensuring that the catch is edible and able to be used;
if fishing for the table, killing them as soon as possible;
if releasing them, giving fish the best chance for future capture and placing all litter including discarded fishing line and empty bait packets into garbage bins.

If today's recreational fishers follow these simple rules quality recreational fishing will continue to be available. There has been an enormous improvement in the attitude and approach of recreational fishers since the late 1980s. Government and the community are increasingly recognising the importance of recreational fishing and making adjustments to commercial fishing to ensure that sufficient fish are available for recreational fishing. We all need to do our part by ensuring that there are enough fish available to reproduce, as poor environmental conditions for recruitment can occur at any time.

This edition is larger and contains information on more fish and how to catch them. The format has also been improved.

I would like to thank the anglers of Australia for their support of the *Australian Fish Guide*.

Please enjoy the book.

Frank Prokop

ALBACORE

Scientific name: Thunnus alalunga. Also known as Tuna (Chicken of the sea).

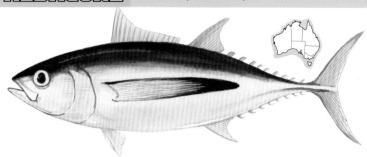

Description: A common species of offshore waters. Average size is 2 to 5 kg but can attain a weight of 30 kilograms. Adults are easily identified by the largest pectoral fin of all tunas, extending well behind the commencement of the second dorsal fin. Juveniles have smaller pectoral fins but the distinctive white rear border of the tail fin differentiates albacore from juvenile yellowfin or bigeye tuna.

Fishing: A good light game fish which fights strongly and requires quality tackle. The albacore readily takes lures such as a feather, minnow or Konahead type lure trolled at around 6 knots. Albacore also take live bait drifted or fished under a bobby cork at a depth of 2.5 to 3 metres.

The albacore is excellent eating, with firm white flesh and a delicate texture.

Rigs and Tactics:

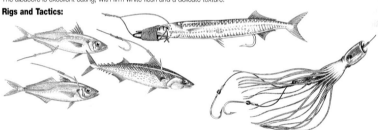

ARCHER FISH

Scientific name: Toxotes chatareus. Also known as Rifle fish.

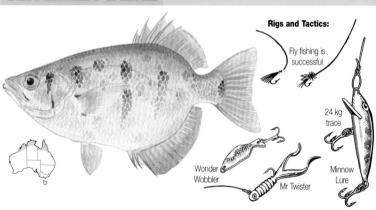

Rigs and Tactics:

Fly fishing is successful

24 kg trace

Wonder Wobbler

Mr Twister

Minnow Lure

Description: A deep bodied fish of tropical freshwater regions. The dorsal fin is set well back, which enables the fish to sit parallel to the surface where it watches for insect life in overhanging branches which it shoots down with a spurt of water from its mouth. They have several large spots on the body and a large, upturned mouth which makes identification relatively easy. While the archer fish may grow to around a kilogram and 30 cm, they are commonly encountered at much smaller sizes.

Fishing: Archer fish are avid takers of lures and flies, often hitting large lures intended for barramundi. They are good fun on light spinning or fly tackle and will take all standard trout flies or lures in larger sizes. Small archer fish make good live baits for barramundi but they are more attractive as aquarium fish, where their water spouting habits make them immensely popular with local kids. Fair eating quality.

AMBERJACK

Scientific name: Seriola dumerili.

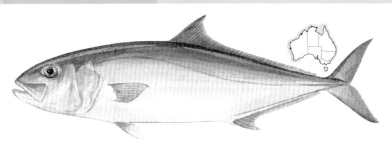

Description: A relatively large, fast swimming species mainly found in offshore waters in the vicinity of reefs or drop-offs. Sometimes confused with yellowtail kingfish, the amberjack has a dark blue to olive tail fin whereas the kingfish has a yellow tail fin. The anal fin of the amberjack is darker in colour with a characteristic white edging. Differs from similar samson fish in having more rays in the dorsal fin (3 –33) versus 23–25 for the samson fish. The samson fish also appears to have red teeth, due to blood engorged gums.

The amberjack attains a weight of 36 kilograms.

Fishing: A hard fighting fish which takes feather or minnow lures trolled near reefs and drop offs. Amberjacks will also take both live and dead bait fished in the vicinity of offshore reefs.

The amberjack makes good eating, although larger specimens tend to be dry and coarse textured.

Rigs and Tactics:

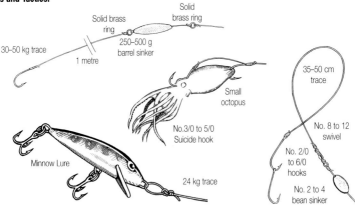

ANCHOVY

Scientific name: Engraulis australis.
Also known as Anchovy, frogmouth pilchard, froggie, Australian anchovy.

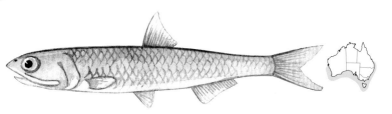

Description: The anchovy is a common bait species which schools in coastal bays and mouths of estuaries and offshore. The pointed fleshy snout and extremely large mouth are characteristic. Grows to 15 cm and is frequently seen smaller in bait shops.

Fishing: A very good bait for fish like flathead and bream. Rig on a single hook or a gang of No 4 to No 1 hooks. Anchovies can be a little soft so they need some care for maximum effectiveness, but the oils which add flavour on pizza also help make this a top bait.

BARRACOUTA

Scientific name: Thyrsites atun. Also known as 'Couta, pickhand axehandle, occasionally by its South African name snoek.

Description: The barracouta is a member of the same family as gemfish (hake) which is a much deeper bodied fish. There is no resemblance to the more tropical barracuda.

The barracouta has a very long first dorsal with a distinctive black patch near the leading edge and around 5 finlets on the caudal peduncle (the gemfish has 2 finlets). The colour is steely grey and the small scales are easily shed. The barracouta has three large teeth on its upper jaw.

Grows to 4.5 kg and 1.3 m but commonly caught at 1–2 kilograms.

Fishing: Barracouta can take a variety of baits and lures. They are frequently taken on chrome spoons or casting lures. Barracouta will also take minnow lures and feathers and soft plastics, but their teeth make short work of all but the most robust lures.

A wire trace will help prevent bite offs of expensive lures and increase the catch rates with baits. Barracouta will take fish flesh, garfish or pilchard baits readily and while partial to live baits are difficult to hook due to a bony mouth and a habit of running with the bait across their jaws.

Barracouta should be handled carefully due to their sharp teeth which also have an anticoagulant which makes any cuts bleed profusely. Barracouta are considered average eating from NSW waters.

Rigs and Tactics:

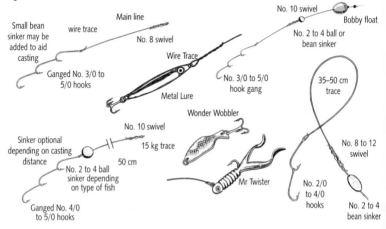

BARRACUDA

Scientific name: Sphyraena barracuda. Also known as Great barracuda, giant barracuda, giant sea pike.

Description: The most remarkable feature of the barracuda is its fearsome teeth. There are two pairs of enlarged canines on the upper jaw and one pair of enlarged canines on the lower jaw. There are other large, backward pointing teeth in both jaws. The body is long and cylindrical with approximately 18 grayish cross bands on the back above the lateral line. These bands on the back and the more heavy body differentiate the barracuda from the similar snook, which is generally found outside of the range of the barracuda. The barracuda reaches 1.8 m and nearly 25 kilograms.

BARRAMUNDI

Scientific name: Lates calcarifer.
Also known as Barra, giant perch.

Description: The barramundi is a special fish which is as beautiful in reality as it is in the dreams of so many anglers. It has a small head with a large mouth and large eyes.

Barramundi have large scales and a particularly powerful tail. Coupled with their thick shoulders, barramundi can put up a good fight, many fish will exhibit the famous gill arching leaps when hooked.

The barramundi can be a brilliant silver colour for sea run fish, ranging to a very dark, chocolate brown colour for fish in billabongs at the end of the dry season or those grown in aquaculture facilities.

Small barra and those in aquaria exhibit a characteristic light stripe down the forehead between the eyes which becomes more pronounced when the fish is excited.

Barramundi in Australia change sex as they grow older (interestingly barramundi in Thailand do not change sex). All fish start out as males and, after spawning once or twice, become female for the rest of their lives. It is therefore impossible to catch a granddaddy barra as it would certainly be female. This sex change is more related to age than size, but barramundi over 8 kg are almost certainly all female.

Rigs and Tactics:

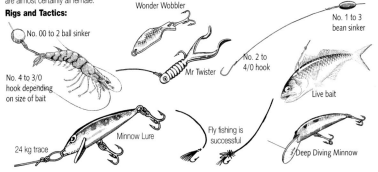

Wonder Wobbler

No. 00 to 2 ball sinker

No. 1 to 3 bean sinker

No. 4 to 3/0 hook depending on size of bait

Mr Twister

No. 2 to 4/0 hook

Live bait

24 kg trace

Minnow Lure

Fly fishing is successful

Deep Diving Minnow

BASS, SAND

Scientific name: Psammoperca waigiensis Also known as Glass-eyed perch, jewel eye, dwarf palmer perch, reef barramundi.

Description: The sand bass has one large flat spine at rear angle of preoperculum. Colour varies from light silvery grey to dark brown; eyes reddish. The lateral line extends onto the caudal fin. Inhabits rocky or coral reefs, frequently in weedy areas, usually in holes and crevices by day. This species can enter estuaries where it can be confused with juvenile barramundi. It can be separated from the barramundi in that the sand bass has granular teeth on the tongue, has a prominent lateral line and only reaches 47 cm but is more common at 30-35 centimetres. The sand bass forages on fishes and crustaceans at night.

Fishing: The sand bass makes good eating, but does not reach the size of its more illustrious cousin the barramundi. Fishing for this species is best adjacent to rocky reefs. The large mouth of the sand bass means that it can be taken on baits intended for other species. The sand bass will take lures or jigs on occasion but they are more widely regarded as a bait species, with cut baits, squid and pilchards.

BASS, AUSTRALIAN

Scientific name: Macquaria novemaculeata.
Also known as Bass, Australian perch.

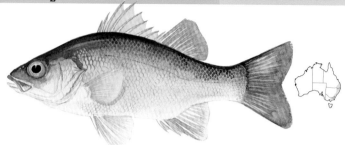

Description: The Australian bass is a handsome fish which can reach more than 4 kg in impoundments, but any fish from the rivers over 2 kg is an extremely noteworthy capture. Males are smaller than females and a large male will be up to 1 kilogram.

The Australian bass is easily confused with the similar estuary perch. Even experts can confuse the two species, but they can be most easily separated by the forehead profile which is straight or slightly rounded in the bass and is concave or slightly indented in the estuary perch.

Fishing: The Australian bass is arguably the best light tackle sportfish of temperate waters in Australia. They have a close affinity for structure and will dash out from their snag to grab a lure, bait or fly and madly dash back into cover, busting off the unwary. Australian bass can be extremely aggressive, feeding on fish, shrimps, prawns, insects, lizards and small snakes.

Australian bass are more active at dusk, dawn or at night. Fishing on a summer's evening is almost unbeatable, with surface lures or popping bugs on a fly rod producing spectacular strikes from dusk and well into the night. Many lures work well and bass anglers have massive collections of surface lures, shallow divers, deep divers, soft plastics, spinnerbaits and special lures in every conceivable pattern and colour.

Rigs and Tactics:

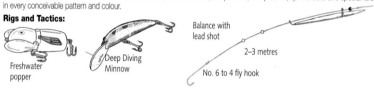

Freshwater popper

Deep Diving Minnow

Balance with lead shot

2–3 metres

No. 6 to 4 fly hook

BASS, RED

Scientific name: Lutjanus bohar
Also known as Two spot red snapper, kelp bream, kelp sea perch.

Caution

☠ **POISONOUS**

The red bass is one of the worst offenders for ciguatera poisoning and should be returned immediately to the water

Description: The red bass is a strikingly coloured fish which can be almost bright orange to a deep brick red. The scales have a paler centre which gives an attractive dappled effect. There is a diagnostic deep groove or channel (often described as a pit) which runs from the nostrils to the front of the eye. The presence of this groove distinguishes the red bass from the similar mangrove jack where larger specimens are also caught on offshore reefs. The snout of the red bass is somewhat pointed. The tail fin is slightly indented and the ventral and anal fins may have a white margin. There is a moderate notch in the preopercular bone. Juvenile and sub-adult red bass have two or sometimes one silvery-white spots on the back, most prominent near the rear of the soft dorsal fin. The red bass can reach 13 kg and a length of 90 centimetres.

Fishing: The red bass inhabits coral reefs, including sheltered lagoons and outer reefs, often adjacent to steep outer reef slopes. Juveniles and some adults can be caught near rocky headlands or near rocky dropoffs. The red bass is usually found singly, but it can be found in small schools, with larger fish showing more solitary tendencies. Red bass are taken with standard reef fishing gear and the standard reef paternoster rig.

Best baits include fresh cut baits, squid, pilchard or other small whole fish. Live baits will attract any predatory reef fish, including red bass. Red bass are also taken on trolled lures intended for species like coral trout. The red bass fights extremely well and will try and bury the unwary angler into any nearby reef. Red bass are totally protected in Queensland.

BONITO

Scientific name: Sarda orientalis. Also known as 'Oriental' Bonito.

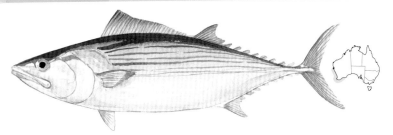

Description: Similar to Australian bonito but differs in separate range and Oriental bonito has no prominent stripes on the lower part of its body. Grows to 3.5 kilograms.

Fishing: Similar methods for Australian bonito. Can be very common in inshore waters, giving a pleasant surprise to shore based casters fishing for tailor and herring. The Oriental bonito should be bled after capture and is only moderately regarded as a food fish.

AUSTRALIAN BONITO

Scientific name: Sarda australis. Also known as Bonny or horse mackerel.

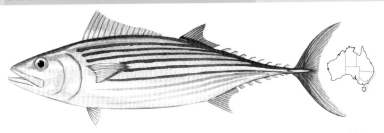

Description: Commonly found in large schools on the coast of Victoria. Easily distinguished from other tunas and bonito species by the presence of narrow horizontal stripes on the lower part of the body. Bonito also have a single row of small but distinct conical teeth. The Australian bonito can grow to 1 m and nearly 8 kg but is usually less than 3 – 4 kilograms.

BONITO, WATSON'S LEAPING

Scientific name: Cybiosarda elegans. Also known as Leaping bonito.

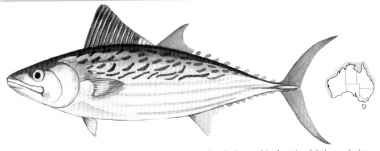

Description: Watson's leaping bonito differs from other bonito as the colouring consists of a series of dusky grey broken lines and blotches above the lateral line and three grayish unbroken lines below the lateral line. It also has a significantly larger first dorsal fin than the other bonito. Reaches a size of approximately 2 kg and 54 centimetres.

Fishing: During winter months the Watson's leaping bonito forms large schools which feed on aggregated baitfish. Schools can be found inshore or on occasions in estuaries. Can be taken on small chrome lures, Christmas tree lures, minnow lures and feather jigs. This species makes terrific cut bait or whole for game species and is better eating than its reputation suggests.

BREAM, BLACK

Scientific name: Acanthopagrus butcheri.
Also known as Bream, blue nosed bream.

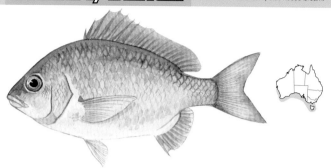

Description: The black bream is a very highly sought after angling species of the estuaries of the southern parts of Australia. The black bream looks very similar to the yellowfin bream and hybrids have been recorded from the Gippsland lakes in Victoria. The major difference is in fin colour, with the black bream possessing brownish or dusky ventral and anal fins. The mouth is fairly small with rows of peg like teeth and crushing plates on the palate. It reaches a maximum size of around 3.5 kg, but a specimen over 1 kg is highly regarded.

Fishing: This is one of the most sought after species in Australia. They are most commonly fished with a light line of 3 – 5 kilograms. Bait running reels on shorter rods are frequently used. Bream generally bite best on a rising tide and after dark but many quality fish, including on lures, are taken during the day and in ambush sites on the bottom half of the tide. Bream can be timid biters so as little weight as possible should be used and any sinker must run freely. Best baits are prawn and yabby, although beach, blood and squirt worms, pipi, anchovy or blue sardine and flesh baits also work extremely well. Some anglers make their own special dough baits out of flour and water with added meat, cheese, sugar, fish oils or other secret ingredients. When bream bite, it is important to let them run up to a metre before setting the hook. The bream will then run strongly for the nearest cover and many fish are lost on this initial surge. They are also excellent lure or soft plastic targets.

Rigs and Tactics:

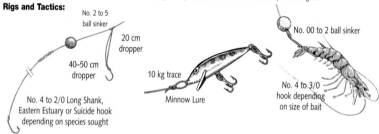

No. 2 to 5 ball sinker

20 cm dropper

40–50 cm dropper

No. 4 to 2/0 Long Shank, Eastern Estuary or Suicide hook depending on species sought

10 kg trace

Minnow Lure

No. 00 to 2 ball sinker

No. 4 to 3/0 hook depending on size of bait

BREAM, PIKEY

Scientific name: Acanthopagrus berda.
Also known as Bream.

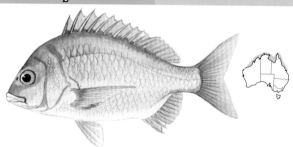

Description: The pikey bream is very similar to the black bream, but with more pointed snout and very stout second anal spine. The pikey bream overlaps in range with the western and eastern yellowfin bream, both of which possess yellow anal and caudal fins. The pikey bream also lacks the characteristic black spot at the base of the pectoral fin of the yellowfin bream. Attains a maximum size of 55 centimetres.

Fishing: Similar methods as for the black bream, but more common around jetties, pylons and creek mouths. The pikey bream makes excellent eating but should be bled and chilled after capture.

BREAM, YELLOWFIN

Scientific name: Acanthopagrus australis. Also known as Silver/Sea/Surf bream.

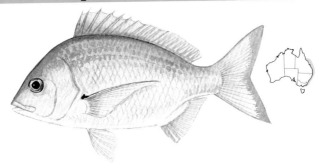

Description: The yellowfin bream is similar to other bream, but with a black spot at the base of the pectoral fin. Also has yellow or yellowish anal and ventral fins. Frequently taken from inshore oceanic waters where the colour is frequently silver, varying to dark olive from estuaries. Lacks the brown horizontal stripes and black stomach cavity lining of the similar tarwhine. Attains a maximum size of 66 cm and 4.4 kg but fish over a kilogram are noteworthy.

Fishing: Fantastic fishing for yellowfin bream can be had near the mouths of estuaries in winter when the fish moves downstream to spawn. Estuarine fish can be taken as described for black bream, with oyster leases, rock walls and edges of drop offs being prime spots. Berley works very well when fish are finicky. Yellowfin bream can be targeted with lightly weighted blue sardines, anchovies or half a pilchard cast into the edge of a good wash. When tailor or tommy rough are feeding, a bait which sinks through the tailor can take some thumping bream.

In the surf, pilchards which repeatedly come back with the gut area eaten out by small bites is a sign that bream may be present, especially if fishing the edges of gutters. A half a pilchard rigged on smaller hooks, a pipi or beach worm bait can take these fish. Bream are excellent lure and soft plastic targets.

Yellowfin bream are excellent eating although fish eating weed can have an iodine taint.

Rigs and Tactics:

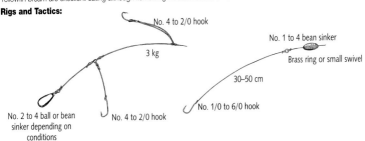

No. 4 to 2/0 hook

3 kg

No. 2 to 4 ball or bean sinker depending on conditions

No. 4 to 2/0 hook

No. 1 to 4 bean sinker

Brass ring or small swivel

30–50 cm

No. 1/0 to 6/0 hook

CALE, ROCK

Scientific name: Crinodus lophodon. Also known as Sea carp, wirrah, weed wirrah, rock cocky, cockatoo fish, cockatoo morwong, marblefish, stinky groper.

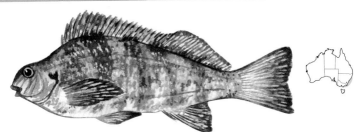

Description: Rock cale are despised by luderick anglers who view them as an inedible and unwelcome by-catch. They can reach 63 centimetres. The rock cale has a small head and a hunched back appearance especially in larger specimens. The rock cale can grow to several kilograms but is commonly encountered at between 0.5 and 1.4 kilograms. All fins are covered with pale spots and the body is blotched and may have indistinct vertical bars. The mouth is small, the lips blubbery and the teeth similar to a luderick's and suited for nipping off weed from the rocks.

CARP

Scientific name: Cyprinus carpio. Also known as European carp, Euro, common carp, koi, blubber lips, mud sucker. Lightly scaled individuals known as mirror carp and those with no or very few scales are known as leather carp.

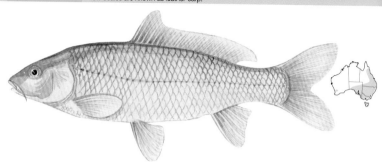

Description: The carp has a relatively small, downward pointing mouth surrounded by two pairs of barbels, with the second pair more prominent. The first spines in the dorsal and anal fins are strongly serrated. Scales may be present, in rows and of a larger size, or almost entirely absent. The decorative koi is a variety of carp and, if released, can breed to wild strain fish capable of much more rapid growth and reproduction. Carp can hybridise with common goldfish (Carassius auratus).

Fishing: Although much maligned, the carp is a powerful fighting fish, especially on light line. Carp are here to stay and in many urban areas provide fishing where little or none was previously available. They can reach 10 kg or more but are more common at 2 – 5 kilograms. Carp can be taken on a wide variety of bait rigs, but coarse fishing techniques elevate carp to a much higher level. The use of coarse fishing gear, rigs and baits such as corn kernels and maggots can account for big bags of carp. Carp take wet flies well and occasionally take lures intended for trout. Carp should not be returned to the water but should not just be left on the banks to rot. Carp are poor eating, although some people do enjoy them, in spite of their frequent muddy taste and large number of Y shaped bones.

Rigs and Tactics:

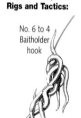

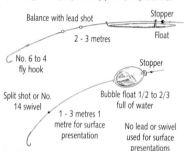

CATFISH, EEL-TAILED

Scientific name: Tandanus tandanus. Also known as Tandan, freshwater jewfish, dewfish, freshwater catfish, kenaru, cattie, tandan catfish.

Description: A fascinating largely nocturnal species with smooth skin and a robust eel-like tail. The eeltailed catfishes' intimidating looks mask a terrific eating and hard fighting fish. The eel-tailed catfish possesses stout and poisonous spines on the dorsal and pectoral fins. The poison is stronger in juvenile catfish for, as the fish grows, the channel along the spine where the poison passes grows over and the spikes become less dangerous in animals over about 20 centimetres. However, the small fish hide in weeds during the day and can spike unwary waders. Immerse the wound in hot water and seek medical advice if swelling or persistent pain cause continued discomfort. These catfish do not possess a true stomach, merely a modification of the intestine. The testes look like fancy scalloping edging and catfish mate in large excavated nests of up to a metre in diameter which they aggressively defend.

CATFISH, FORKTAIL

Scientific name: Arius graeffei. Also known as Salmon catfish, blue catfish, sea catfish.

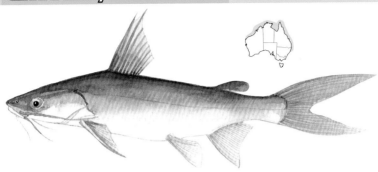

Description: These catfish are quite remarkable in that the males hold the large yolky eggs in their mouths until the eggs hatch. The underside of the skull when dried produces a crucifix like structure. The various forktail catfish are difficult to differentiate. The giant salmon catfish (Arius leptaspis) grows to over 1.1 m as opposed to 69 cm for the blue catfish. The giant catfish has dorsal and pectoral spines which are the same length. Another similar species is marketed as silver cobbler (Arius midgleyi) and reaches weights of 15 kg in Lake Argyle. This species was very rare before the construction of the dam.

Fishing: Fork tailed catfish are held in low esteem by many anglers. This is largely as they are often taken while fishing for more prized species like barramundi, queenfish or mangrove jack, taking live baits or creating a false expectation when a lure is hit. Catfish will take baits and lures very well. They have a particular preference for cut baits. Larger forktail catfish fight well and the eating qualities of catfish from clean water is higher than generally believed, as the market acceptance of silver cobbler will attest.

CATFISH, ESTUARY

Scientific name: Cnidoglanis macrocephalus. Also known as Cobbler.

Description: A very long eel-tailed species found in muddy or weedy estuaries. They are most commonly caught near washed up weeds or near weed patches. When spawning, cobbler form balls of fish which can be spotted by the muddy water which surrounds them. They make nests in weed.

The pectoral and dorsal fins possess a large spine which contains a poison gland. A puncture wound causes a great deal of pain. Treatment is with hot water or compresses to cook the protein.

Fishing: Cobbler are actively fished for in many areas with light bottom rigs and baits of prawn or worms. They are good fighters but must be handled carefully when being unhooked. In some areas, estuary catfish are taken by gidgee or spear in the shallows at night. In spite of their appearance, estuary catfish are excellent eating and are highly prized in Western Australia.

Rigs and Tactics:

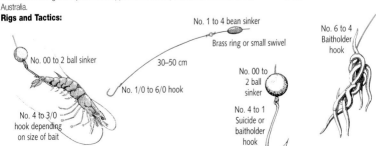

No. 00 to 2 ball sinker

No. 4 to 3/0 hook depending on size of bait

No. 1 to 4 bean sinker

Brass ring or small swivel

30–50 cm

No. 1/0 to 6/0 hook

No. 00 to 2 ball sinker

No. 4 to 1 Suicide or baitholder hook

No. 6 to 4 Baitholder hook

CHINAMAN FISH

Scientific name: Symphorus nematophorus. Also known as Threadfin sea perch (juveniles), galloper. Do not confuse with Chinaman cod, a common and safe catch in north WA.

Caution

POISONOUS

Description: Juveniles look substantially different from adults with blue stripes on a yellow background and extended soft dorsal ray filaments. Fins are reddish pink. Adults lack extended filaments and are reddish with dark vertical bars. Adults have a stout body and a row of scales on the cheeks. The Chinaman fish also possesses a deep pit on the upper snout, immediately before the eyes.

CHERABIN

Scientific name: Machrobracium rosenbergii
Also known as cherubin, cherrabin, freshwater prawn.

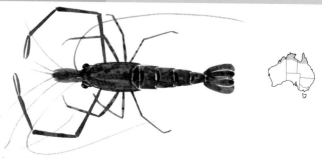

Description: A large freshwater and upper estuarine shrimp that is capable of reaching around 300 grams. The cherabin can be a deep translucent blue to a brown depending on the clarity of the water. Cherabin have a characteristic pair of very long, slender but remarkably flexible nippers that can be a dark brown or almost black. The nippers do not look like they can do much damage, but they can really give a painful nip. There is a similar species (Machrobrachium australiense) which is found in the Murray Darling drainage which reaches around 15 cm in body length.
Fishing: The cherabin is considered to be excellent eating and although it is an absolutely first rate live bait and almost as good a dead bait, many do not make it into the bait bucket and are consumed in their own right. Cherabin are taken in throw nets and can be berleyed up with small bits of meat or unscented soap flakes. Cherabin can be taken in bait traps or an old paint tin with holes in it and a piece of meat hung in the neck of the tin set in a deeper hole. One of the best baits is a piece of Sunlight or other unscented soap which works surprisingly well. Cherabin can also be taken with a scoop net and a torch at night when they are much more active.
Rigs and Tactics: Baits, throw net, bait trap or paint tin trap.

COBIA

Scientific name: MRachycentron canadus.
Also known as Cobe, black kingfish, black king, crab-eater, sergeant fish, lemon fish.

Description: A large pelagic species reaching over 2 m and 60 kilograms. Frequently mistaken initially for a shark in the water due to its high dorsal fin and large, dark pectoral fins. Often found with manta rays.
They have a relatively pointy head with the mouth at the middle of the front of the head. They have a white or creamy belly and a white stripe on their sides which may fade after death. They also have very short dorsal spines before the high soft dorsal fin. Other fins, except pelvic are dark and the overall colour is chocolate brown to black.

COD, BLACK

Scientific name: Epinephelus daemelii.

Description: Found on offshore reefs, occasionally found in estuaries. Young fish are mottled grey with six vivid vertical bands. When fully grown they are capable of rapid colour changes, but retain a dark patch just above the tail. Grows to 45 kilograms.

COD, BREAKSEA

Scientific name: Epinephelides armatus.
Also known as Black-arse cod, black arse, tiger cod.

Description: Relatively common inshore species often found around bommies and shallow reefs. Colour varies but can be brown to yellow with dusky black fins. The eye is a bright red and the anus is found in a large black spot, leading to the common names.

Fishing: This species is commonly taken in mixed reef catches. Breaksea cod have a large mouth and will take large baits intended for other species. Standard reef paternoster rigs and baits work well with cut baits, prawn, pilchard and squid working well. This species is good eating.

Rigs and Tactics:

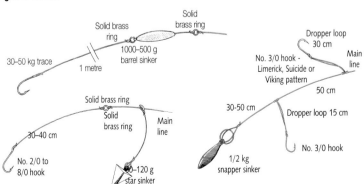

COD, CHINAMAN

Scientific name: Epinephelus rivulatus.
Also known as Chinaman rockcod, Charlie Court cod.

Description: A fairly small but attractive cod species with the fairly typical large mouth and long dorsal fin with lobed soft dorsal. The Chinaman cod can be distinguished by 4 or 5 prominent broad bars down the sides, although these can be very pale in specimens taken near sandy or broken bottoms. There are frequently white blotches on the head. The Chinaman cod is similar to the black-tipped rockcod, but lacks the distinctive black to reddish tips to the dorsal spines. The Chinaman cod reaches 45 cm and around 1.3 kg but is frequently caught at around 30 centimetres.

Fishing: The Chinaman cod is a common table catch in the north-west of the state. It is taken on standard reef rigs and baits of cut fish, pilchard, squid and octopus. In places like Ningaloo Reef, the Chinaman cod is a common capture which makes pleasant eating and compensates for the times when north-west snapper and other more prized fish are less accommodating. Chinaman cod are most frequently taken from deeper reefs where the heavier lines and larger hooks tend to sandbag a reasonable fight.

Rigs and Tactics:

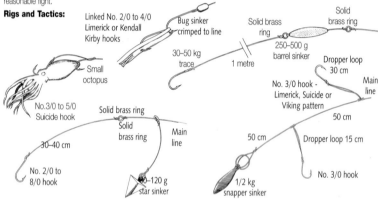

COD, EASTERN FRESHWATER

Scientific name: Maccullochella ikei.
Also known as Clarence River cod,
Eastern cod, cod.

Description: Closely related to the Murray cod but distinguished by range, Eastern Freshwater cod also possess long leading filaments on ventral fin. Eastern Freshwater cod are more lightly built than Murray cod, especially near the tail and have heavier mottling patterns.

Fishing: Classic ambush feeder living near cover in deep holes in beautiful clear streams. Takes deep and surface lures and large live baits. The fight is strong and there is inevitably a surge when the boat or angler is first sighted and the danger realised. This species is totally protected and if accidently taken must be returned immediately to the water.

COD, ESTUARY

Scientific name: Epinephelus coioides. Also known as Greasy cod, spotted cod, north-west groper, estuary rock cod, gold spotted rock cod, spotted river cod, orange-spotted cod.

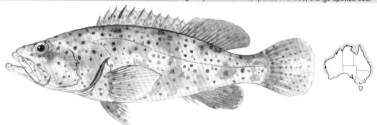

Description: The Estuary Cod is Frequently misidentified as Epinephelus malabaricus or Epinephelus tauvina. The estuary cod is one of the largest and most common cod found in tropical estuaries and coastal reefs reaching a length of over 2 m and 230 kilograms. The estuary cod is olivegreen to brown with scattered brown spots. The back has four to six darker blotches which fade with age to uniform brown colour. Similar to Queensland groper but the estuary cod has three opercular spines equal distances apart. The tail is rounded.

COD, FLOWERY

Scientific name: Epinephelus fuscoguttatus. Also known as carpet cod, black rock-cod

Description: A heavy bodied cod species, the flowery cod generally has a fairly pale brown colour with darker chocolate brown 'flower' blotches on the sides. There are also numerous smaller spots over the body, including the stomach and the fins. The tail fin is heavily spotted and rounded while the spots on the ventral fins are an unusual feature of several closely related species.

Juvenile flowery cod up to around 4 kg are often found in northern mangrove creeks. Adults are found on offshore reefs or on broken ground near reefs. This species can reach 90 cm while the small toothed cod reaches 63 centimetres.

COD, MARY RIVER

Scientific name: Maccullochella peeli mariensis. Also known as Cod, Queensland freshwater cod.

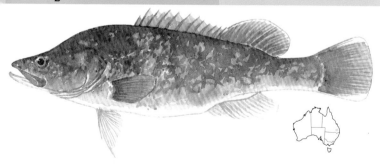

Description: Similar to Eastern Freshwater cod, but more closely related to the Murray cod. Easily separated by the limited range.

Fishing: Takes lures and baits within its limited range. This species is at risk and should be returned regardless of the prevailing regulations.

COD, MURRAY

Scientific name: Maccullochella peelii peelii.
Also known as Cod, goodoo, green fish, codfish, ponde.

Description: The Murray cod is the largest Australian freshwater fish, reaching 1.8 m and 113 kilograms. Cod grow an average of 1 kg per year in rivers and 2 kg per year in larger dams. Has prominent mottling on body, reducing towards a white or cream belly. Fin borders except pectoral fins are white. Differs from similar trout cod in having lower jaw equal or longer than upper jaw, more prominent mottling and heavier tail wrist. Murray cod also prefer more sluggish water than trout cod.

Fishing: Murray cod are the largest predator in many inland waters. They take large lures, especially deep divers cast to snags or drop-offs in larger, slower rivers or dams. Murray cod are now a legitimate target for keen fly fishers. Murray cod reward patience, as a lure repeatedly cast to cod holding cover, or to a following fish will often eventually evoke a strike. As Murray cod are ambush feeders, large or flashy lures often work best.

Murray cod are best known for taking a wide range of baits including live fish (where permitted), bardi grubs, yabbies, worms, ox heart and even scorched starlings. Murray cod are very good eating, especially under 10 kilograms. Anglers should only take as many cod as they need.

Rigs and Tactics:

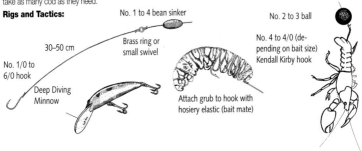

No. 1 to 4 bean sinker

No. 2 to 3 ball

30–50 cm

Brass ring or small swivel

No. 4 to 4/0 (depending on bait size) Kendall Kirby hook

No. 1/0 to 6/0 hook

Deep Diving Minnow

Attach grub to hook with hosiery elastic (bait mate)

COD, VERMICULAR

Scientific name: Plectropomus oligocanthus.
Also known as lined coral trout, vermicular trout.

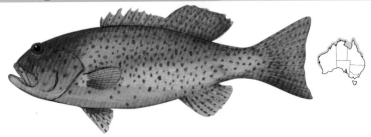

Description: The various coral trout species being coral trout, bar-cheek coral trout and vermicular cod are all easily confused. The vermicular cod tends to be more bright red or orange red, while coral trout can be a dark brick red. The vermicular cod has larger blue dots on its body and some are likely to be elongated dorsally. The spots on the head are fewer and larger than with the coral trout and are not elongated laterally as with the bar-cheek coral trout. The vermicular cod also has a higher soft part of the dorsal fin, but this characteristic is most useful when comparing another trout. The vermicular cod is found on off-shore reefs more commonly and reaches 56 cm in length whereas the coral trout reaches 75 cm and the bar-cheek coral trout 70 centimetres.

Fishing: Like all the coral trouts, the vermicular cod is first rate eating. It is taken on standard reef fishing rigs. Its preference for coral reefs and a strong first run makes heavier line more necessary. The vermicular cod will also rise to take trolled lures and bait tipped jigs also work extremely well. Best baits include cut fish baits, pilchard, garfish, squid, octopus and large prawns.

DART, SWALLOWTAIL

Scientific name: Trachinotus botla.
Also known as Dart, Common Dart,
Swallowtail, Southern swallowtail

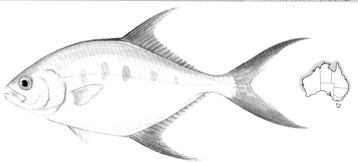

Description: From the same family as trevally, the swallowtail dart bears some external similarities and shares the same tenacious side-on fight. Dart are handsome fish with a deeply forked tail. The dorsal fin is set well back on the fish and the first few dorsal and anal rays are elongated. The swallowtail dart has between one and five large spots on the side of the fish. The swallowtail dart is distinguished from the black spotted dart whose spots are smaller than the pupil of the eye. The snub nosed dart has no spots on its sides and a much more blunt, rounded head profile.

The swallowtail dart grows to 60 cm but is often caught at smaller sizes. A dart of larger than 1 kg is noteworthy, and their strong fight makes up for their lack of size.

DHUFISH

Scientific name: Glaucosoma hebraicum.
Also known as Westralian dhufish, jewfish, dhuie, jewie.

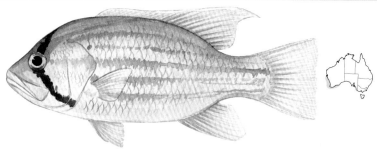

Description: The dhufish is an attractive relative of the pearl perch, and is the most prized species for Western Australian boat anglers. The dhufish has a distinctive eye stripe. A dorsal ray, especially in males can be elongated. Juvenile dhufish have distinctive horizontal black stripes. It is found in depths of up to 140 m or so. Recent research indicates high mortality of fish taken in greater than 50 m or so but using depth release sinkers to rapidly return the fish to depth is strongly recommended. Dhufish have a very large mouth and can take a big bait. Dhufish can reach 27 kg and every year a number of fish of 22 kg are taken.

Fishing: Tagging studies show very limited movement of dhufish. Dhufish take baits fished on standard deep water two hook rigs. They take whole fish, squid, pilchard or live fish if available. Whiting heads are a favourite bait. Anglers drift lumps in waters from 10 – 70 m in depth for mixed bags with dhufish the most prized species. Taken from deep water, a big dhufish feels like the bottom, but the fight diminishes as the fish nears the surface. This fish is arguably the best eating species in Western Australia.

Rigs and Tactics:

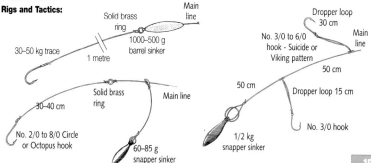

DORY, JOHN

Scientific name: Zeus faber.
Also known as St Peter's fish, doorkeeper's fish, dory keparu (NZ).

Description: An unusual fish with a large, upward pointing mouth which can be extended the length of its head. The John dory has a distinctive, prominent mark on each side, said to be made by the fingers of St Peter when he picked up this fish. The John dory has very fine scales compared with the mirror dory which has no scales. The elongated dorsal rays give a distinctive appearance. John dory are most common near mid to deepwater reefs from 10 to 80 m but can be found in deeper estuaries. The John dory can reach 75 cm and 4 kg although they are commonly taken at around a kilogram.

Fishing: The John dory is a poor fighter but it is absolutely delicious. The John dory is a common deep water trawl species in temperate waters but can be taken by anglers near deep reefs, wrecks and in deep estuaries such as the Hawkesbury. John dory greatly prefer live fish such as yellowtail for bait but can be caught on very fresh fillets.

Rigs and Tactics:

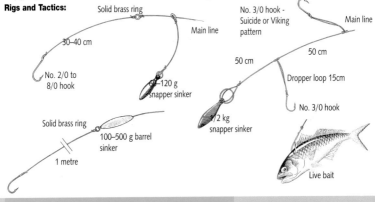

DART, SNUB-NOSED

Scientific name: Trachinotus blochii.
Also known as Oyster cracker, permit.

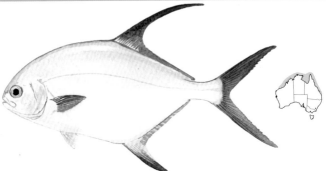

Description: The snub-nosed dart possesses similar characteristics to the swallow-tail dart with elongated sickle shaped dorsal and anal fins. The snub-nosed dart has characteristic orange or yellow colouration of the ventral and anal fins. This fish has quite a small mouth and the nose is rounded. The eye is quite large and close to the mouth. The snub-nosed dart can reach a size of 65 cm and more than 9 kilograms.

DRUMMER, BLACK

Scientific name: Girella elevata. Also known as Rock blackfish, Eastern rock blackfish, pig, black tank.

Description: The black drummer is a deep bodied and incredibly powerful fish. While the black drummer can have mottled colouring in some circumstances, it is often a uniform black colour and never possesses the distinctive vertical stripes of the luderick. The head and mouth is small and the profile rounded. There are 13 spines in the dorsal of the rock blackfish compared with 14–16 in the luderick and 11 in the silver drummer.

Fishing: This is a strong, dirty fighter who lives close to the rocks and reefs which it will dive into to break off any poorly prepared angler. Black drummer are often encountered by anglers fishing for luderick with delicate gear and light traces which are no match for a large 'pig'. Rock blackfish are often taken on cabbage weed. Cunjevoi and peeled prawn make good bait, but every picker in the area will attack the bait, especially on the edges of the white water. Black drummer can also be taken on bread. With cabbage and bread, berley is an advantage but do not berley so much that the fish can fill up. Other baits include crab portion, abalone gut, and occasionally squid and cuttlefish. Extra strong hooks are recommended.

Rigs and Tactics:

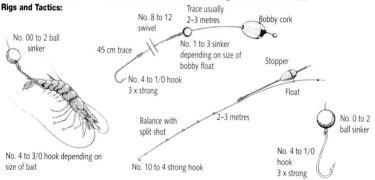

DRUMMER, SILVER

Scientific name: Kyphosus cornelii. Also known as western buffalo bream, buffie.

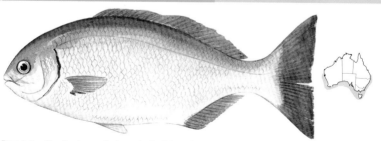

Description: The silver drummer is a large schooling fish growing to 12 kg which offers better sport than eating. These mainly herbivorous fish are found in surge zones and near inshore reefs. They are dusky silver with fairly prominent lengthwise bands. The lips appear more prominent than in rock blackfish and the head is more pointed.

Fishing: Silver drummer are fished for with sea cabbage, bread, and prawns. They can take bluebait or pilchards intended for other species. Silver drummer are caught under floats in the surge zones or on lightly weighted baits fished near inshore reefs. Berley of bread, or weed works well.

Silver drummer fight hard but fair and make poor eating even if bled and cleaned immediately. Be careful when handling the silver drummer as it often defecates when anglers try to unhook it.

EMPEROR, BLUE SPOT

Scientific name: Lethrinus laticaudis.

Also known as grass emperor, grass sweetlip, coral bream, snapper bream, grey sweetlip, red-finned emperor, brown sweetlip

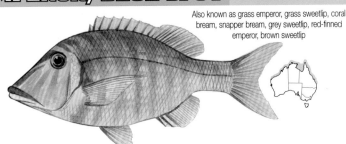

Description: The various species of spangled emperors are difficult to differentiate. Many of the species have different size limits and must be able to be separated to comply with various state fishing regulations.

The blue spot emperor is a common capture in tropical waters and is often caught near weed beds. Juveniles in particular can be caught near beds of eel-grass (Zostera sp.). The blue lined emperor grows to an impressive 80cm, which is nearly as large as the spangled emperor. The species can be most easily separated by the blue spots on the cheeks, as opposed to blue bars on the spangled emperor.

EMPEROR, LONG NOSED

Scientific name: Lethrinus olivaceous.

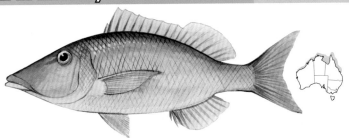

Description: One of the largest species of emperor, reaching 10 kg and a metre in length. Easily distinguished by the long sloping head and the generally greenish colouration. There is generally a red line on the lips of these fish and the dorsal fin may have red spots.

Fishing: Standard reef fishing tackle and rigs will account for this hard fighting species. Can be found on inshore or offshore reefs and its larger size can cause extra troubles for angling. Fresh baits and strong leaders are recommended. Fish flesh, squid, octopus, pilchard or live baits account for the majority of these fish. Highly regarded as a food fish.

EMPEROR, SWEETLIP

Scientific name: Lethrinus miniatus. (formerly Lethrinus chrysostomus) Also known as Sweetlip, lipper, red-throat.

Description: The sweetlip emperor is a common emperor species. It is identified by orange areas around the eyes, a bright red dorsal fin, and a red patch at the base of the pectoral fins. The inside of the mouth is red. Some fish have a series of brown vertical bands but many fish are a uniform colour. This species reaches a metre and 9 kg but is more common from 1 to 2.5 kilograms.

Fishing: Found in reef country, but frequently taken from areas between reefs, the sweetlip emperor can be berleyed up and large catches taken from the feeding school. The sweetlip emperor fights well and is able to dive to the bottom and break off an unwary angler. Sweetlip emperor are highly regarded food fish.

EMPEROR, SPANGLED

Scientific name:
Lethrinus nebulosus.

Also known as Nor-west snapper, Nor'wester, yellow sweetlip, sand snapper, sand bream.

Description: A striking member of the sweetlip group. This species is easily identified by the blue spots on each scale and the blue bars on the cheek. This species can reach 86 cm and 6.5 kg and is considered very good eating.

Fishing: The spangled emperor is generally taken adjacent to coral or rock reefs over gravel or sand bottoms. They frequent lagoons and coral cays and can be taken from the beach in Western Australia where there are reef patches nearby. They are particularly active at night.

The spangled emperor can be taken with standard reef rigs, but as they are most common in water under 15 metres deep, lighter rigs and berley can bring these fish up into the open. Use cut fish, pilchards, squid, octopus, crab or prawn baits. Spangled emperor will take jigs or minnow lures either trolled or cast in areas near reefs where spangled emperor feed.

Rigs and Tactics:

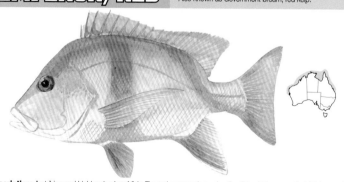

No. 3/0 hook - Suicide or Viking pattern

Main line

50 cm

50 cm

Dropper loop 15cm

No. 3/0 Hook

1/2 kg snapper sinker

Linked No. 2/0 to 5/0 Kendall Kirby hooks

Bug sinker crimped to line

Solid brass ring

Solid brass ring

30–50 kg trace

1 metre

250–500 g barrel sinker

EMPEROR, RED

Scientific name: Lutjanus sebae.
Also known as Government bream, red kelp.

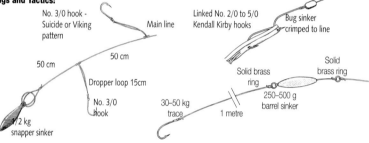

Description: A striking and highly prized reef fish. The red emperor is a schooling fish which means that fishing can be fast and furious, but this valuable species can be taken in large numbers in commercial fish traps and trawls.

The red emperor changes appearance as it grows. Juveniles are known as Government bream as the three striking bands resemble a convict's broad arrow. This pattern fades with age and fish over 13 kg become a uniform scarlet or salmon pink. The reddish fins are narrowly edged with white. The cheeks are scaled and there is a deep notch in the lower edge of the pre-operculum (inner cheekbone).

Fishing: Red emperor fight extremely well, even when taken from deeper waters where they are increasingly taken. The red emperor can reach 22 kg and more than a metre in length which increases their allure.

Red emperor prefer moving water in channels near deeper reefs. As a result, they can be taken on drifts between reef patches in seemingly open ground. They tend to form schools of similar sized fish and are partial to cut fish baits, octopus, squid or pilchards. The red emperor is excellent eating even in the larger sizes and is considered safe from ciguatera.

EEL, LONG-FINNED

Scientific name: Anguilla reinhardtii.
Also known as Freshwater eel, eel, spotted eel.

Description: Eels are fascinating animals which are often loathed but play an important part in culling older or sick fish, birds or anything else they can catch. Australian eels are thought to spawn in the Coral Sea. Juvenile eels as elvers migrate great distances up rivers and can travel overland over wet grass and can negotiate large dams walls. Long-finned eels can spend more than 10 years in fresh waters until the urge to move downstream takes the adult eels.

The long-finned eel is much larger than the short-finned eel (Anguilla australis) and has the dorsal fin extending well forward of the anal fin. The head is broad and the lips fleshy. Colour varies with the environment but, except when migrating to the sea, is brown or olive-green with a lighter belly.

Fishing: The long-finned eel is often taken while fishing for other fish. They fight extremely hard and can be mean enough to try to bite the hand which tries to unhook it. The long-finned eel can demonstrate knot tying tricks when hooked. These eels are opportunistic feeders and can take live baits larger than the 10% of the body length which legend believes applies. Worms, grubs, live fish or cut baits will take eels, but liver and beef heart are irresistible. Long-finned eels can reach over 2 m and 20 kg, although divers claim much larger sizes in some dams. Eels make good eating, especially when smoked, although many Australians are strongly prejudiced against them. Large eels gain a top price in China, whereas smaller eels are more popular in Japan.

Rigs and Tactics:

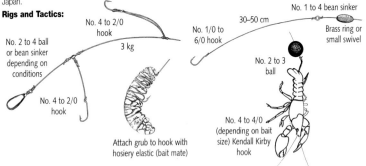

No. 2 to 4 ball or bean sinker depending on conditions

No. 4 to 2/0 hook

No. 4 to 2/0 hook

3 kg

Attach grub to hook with hosiery elastic (bait mate)

30–50 cm

No. 1/0 to 6/0 hook

No. 1 to 4 bean sinker

Brass ring or small swivel

No. 2 to 3 ball

No. 4 to 4/0 (depending on bait size) Kendall Kirby hook

EEL, COMMON PIKE

Scientific name: Muraenesox bagio
Also known as pike eel, silver eel.

Description: The pike eel is similar to the conger eels, the short finned conger-eel (Conger wilsoni) and the Southern conger-eel (Conger verreauxi) but the common pike eel has a longer jaw and sharp teeth. The gill opening is set back form the mouth and just in front of the pectoral fins. The dorsal fin commences in front of the pectoral fins whereas with the congers, the dorsal fin commences behind the pectoral fins. The upper jaw of the common pike eel can be hooked and notched to accommodate some pretty nasty teeth in the front of the lower jaw. The common pike eel grows to 1.5 m and is most commonly found in muddy estuaries or near seagrasses which have a mud or silt/sand bottom nearby. They can be found in quite deep water in these estuaries but are rarely taken from open ocean waters.

Fishing: This is one species of fish which can be particularly nasty when captured. They are frequently taken while drifting deeper water in estuaries for flathead, bream or mulloway. A large common pike eel when taken into a boat, will thrash around, rearing onto its tail and lash out with its vicious teeth, biting everything within reach at random. These fish are also extremely hardy and can take a long time to become subdued. A far better tactic is to cut the common pike eel off beside the boat, sacrificing a hook but potentially saving the relationship with all others in the boat. The common pike eel is quite a large species and its impressive fight gives rise to hopes of an extremely large dusky flathead instead of an attacking eel. The common pike eel will take most baits, with live baits, cut baits, pilchard, whitebait, prawns and squid all taking fish. The pike eel is regarded as quite good eating, but very few make it to the table given their unfortunate habit of trying to bite the hand that fed it.

ELEPHANT FISH

Scientific name: Callorhynchus milii. Also known as Elephant shark, ghost shark, whitefish, plownose chimera.

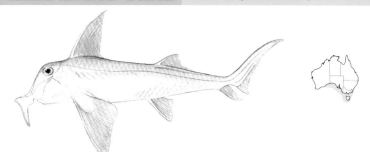

Description: The elephant fish is a unique species easily recognised by the fleshy nose which is used to find food in sandy or lightly silted bottoms. The pectoral fins are large and used like a ray for navigation. The eggs are spindle shaped, about 20 cm long and take 8 months to hatch.

Unlike most sharks, the elephant fish has a single gill slit. It has a prominent dorsal spine like a Port Jackson shark and can inflict a painful wound if not handled carefully.

Fishing: Until recently, these fish were shunned due to their ugly appearance. However, the flesh is white and firm and good eating and they are being increasingly targeted in southern bays and inlets in summer. Light bottom rigs get maximum sport from these fish. However it is important to realise that the summer fishery targets spawning fish and the take of these fish should be limited to ensure that they are not over-exploited.

Rigs and Tactics:

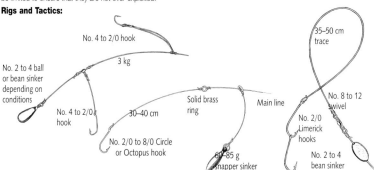

No. 4 to 2/0 hook

3 kg

No. 2 to 4 ball or bean sinker depending on conditions

No. 4 to 2/0 hook

30–40 cm

No. 2/0 to 8/0 Circle or Octopus hook

Solid brass ring

Main line

60–85 g snapper sinker

35–50 cm trace

No. 8 to 12 swivel

No. 2/0 Limerick hooks

No. 2 to 4 bean sinker

FINGERMARK

Scientific name: Lutjanus johnii. Also known as Fingermark bream, big scale red, golden snapper.

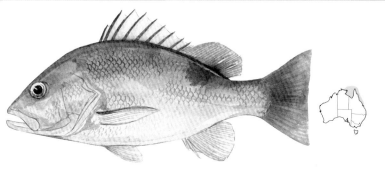

Description: The fingermark is a large sea-perch commonly taken from northern inshore and reef waters and estuaries. It has a speckled appearance because of a dark spot on each scale, which gives the appearance of parallel fine stripes. A large black blotch which varies in colour and intensity is located below the soft dorsal rays. Grows to 90 cm and more than 10 kilograms.

FLATHEAD, BAR-TAIL

Scientific name: Platycephalus endrachtensis. Also known as Western estuary flathead.

Description: The bar tail flathead can be readily identified by the tail fin which has black and white horizontal stripes on the tail with a yellow blotch at the top of the fin. The similar northern sand flathead which grows to 45 cm has similar tail colouration but no yellow blotch. The bar-tail flathead is found on sand, gravel, light rock and silt bottoms.

The bar-tailed flathead is reported as reaching 1 m in length, but in the Swan estuary where it is particularly targeted, any fish above 55 cm is noteworthy and most fish are between 30 and 45 centimetres.

FLATHEAD, DUSKY

Scientific name: Platycephalus fuscus. Also known as Estuary flathead, mud flathead, black flathead, flattie, frog and lizard.

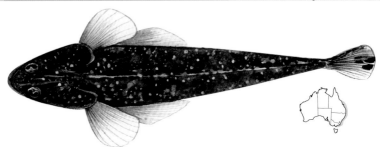

Description: The dusky flathead is the largest of the 30 species of flathead in Australia, reaching 10 kg and 150 centimetres. Any fish above 5 kg is certainly worth boasting about. The flathead shape is unmistakable, and the dusky flathead also has the sharp opercular (cheek) spines to spike the unwary. The colouration is highly variable from light fawn to black depending on the type of bottom they are found on. The belly ranges from creamy yellow to white.

The tail fin features a characteristic dark spot in the top end corner and a patch of blue on the lower half. This is an estuarine or inshore species. This feature plus its large size and good eating make it the ultimate prize for many weekend anglers.

Rig and Tactics:

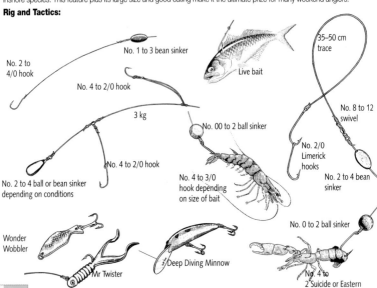

No. 2 to 4/0 hook

No. 1 to 3 bean sinker

Live bait

35–50 cm trace

No. 4 to 2/0 hook

3 kg

No. 8 to 12 swivel

No. 4 to 2/0 hook

No. 00 to 2 ball sinker

No. 2 to 4 ball or bean sinker depending on conditions

No. 4 to 3/0 hook depending on size of bait

No. 2/0 Limerick hooks

No. 2 to 4 bean sinker

Wonder Wobbler

Mr Twister

Deep Diving Minnow

No. 0 to 2 ball sinker

No. 4 to 2 Suicide or Eastern Estuary hook

FLATHEAD, EASTERN BLUE SPOT

Scientific name: Platycephalus caeruleopuntatus. Also known as Blue-spotted flathead, drift flathead, longnose flathead, red spotted flathead.

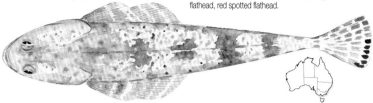

Description: Flathead identification can be quite difficult, but the Eastern blue spot flathead has three or four black ovals or bars on the lower part of the tail fin. This species is generally found at a length of less than 45 centimetres. The eastern blue spot flathead is a common catch on the near shore sand banks of NSW with fish, prawns and pilchards being very popular baits.

FLATHEAD, SOUTHERN BLUE SPOT

Scientific name: Platycephalus speculator. Also known as Southern flathead, yank flathead, Castelnau's flathead, southern dusky flathead, bluespot flathead, long nose flathead, shovelnose flathead.

Description: This flathead can be distinguished on the basis of grey-green spots on the top half of the tail and 3 to 5 large black spots on the lower portion, surrounded by white or off-white. This species also has only one dorsal spine compared with two for many other flathead. The southern blue-spotted flathead can reach a maximum size of nearly 8 kg, although any fish of 3 kg is rare and it is much more common at around a kilogram.

Fishing: The southern blue-spot flathead ambushes prey wherever possible. This species can occasionally be found over weed patches or around the edges of weeds. It is not as commonly taken on lures and can be a welcome bonus when fishing for King George whiting or when baits sink through berley fishing for herring and garfish. The southern blue-spotted flathead is good eating.

FLATHEAD, SAND

Scientific name: latycephalus arenarius (Northern), Platycephalus bassensis (Southern).

Also known as flag tailed flathead in the North; slimy flathead, bay flathead, common flathead, sandy flathead in the South.

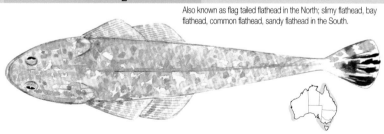

Description: The various sand flatheads are generally smaller than the blue-spotted or dusky flathead. The northern sand flathead can reach 45 cm but is more commonly encountered in large numbers at around 30 cm in estuaries or on adjacent beaches. They can be found to a depth of 30 fathoms. They have a distinctive pattern of long, horizontal black stripes on its tail. The southern sand flathead has two or sometimes three squared off black patches on the lower part of the tail fin. This species is reputed to reach over 3 kg but is rarely found over a kilogram.

Fishing: These fish are taken with similar methods for other flathead. The northern sand flathead will move upwards a greater distance to take a lure than the other flathead. These fish can be found with other flathead species and can be a pest at smaller sizes, seemingly being all mouth and spines and picking apart baits intended for tailor, bream or large dusky flathead that can all be found in similar areas. They are good eating and are undervalued.

FLATHEAD, TIGER

Scientific name: Neoplatycephalus richardsoni. Also known as Trawl flathead, king flathead, spiky flathead, toothy flathead.

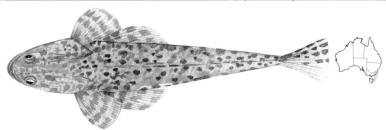

Description: Tiger flathead have a somewhat more cylindrical body compared to the obviously compressed form of the other flathead. Tiger flathead colour varies but generally has a reddish-orange or reddish-brown base colour but with brighter orange spots which extend to the tail. The tiger flathead has large teeth on the roof of mouth. The maximum size is 2.5 kg but they are most often encountered from 0.5 to 1.5 kilograms.

Fishing: Tiger flathead are a common trawl species in the south-eastern waters to a depth of 80 fathoms. However, in parts of Victoria and Tasmania they can enter bays, harbours and estuaries. As they are often taken from deep water, heavy handlines or boat rods and typical paternoster rigs with up to four droppers are used. Baits of fish flesh, pilchards, squid or prawns take most fish. In shallower water, live baits prove deadly. Tiger flathead are a highly regarded food fish.

Rigs and Tactics:

No. 2 to 4/0 hook

No. 1 to 3 bean sinker

Dropper loop 30 cm

Main line

No. 3/0 hook - Limerick, Suicide or Viking pattern

No. 2 to 5 ball sinker

40–50 cm dropper

20 cm dropper

50 cm

50 cm

Dropper loop 15 cm

No. 4 to 2/0 Long Shank, Eastern Estuary or Suicide hook depending on species sought

1/2 kg snapper sinker

No. 3/0 hook

FLOUNDER, GREENBACK

Scientific name: Rhombosolea tapirina. Also known as Melbourne flounder, southern flounder.

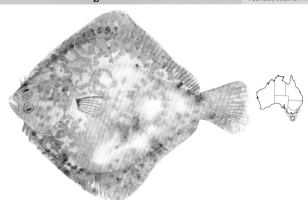

Description: Scientific name: Description: The greenback flounder is a right eyed flounder which reaches 0.6 kilograms. It is distinguished from the long snouted flounder by the overall kite-like shape caused by the dorsal and anal fins tapering down to a more triangular shape. The head is also more pointed as it lacks the fleshy snout of the long snouted flounder. This species enters shallow waters on the rising tide at night.

Fishing: Where permitted this excellent eating fish is taken by hand spear. Otherwise small lightly weighted baits fished across sand or sand/mud flats at night can take these fish. They are a welcome catch while fishing for other species such as bream and whiting at other times and in deeper water.

FLOUNDER, LARGE TOOTHED

Scientific name: Pseudorhombus arsius. Also known as Flounder.

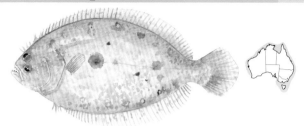

Description: The large toothed flounder is a left eyed flounder, i.e. both eyes are on the left side after the right eye migrates around the head during juvenile development. This species has highly variable colouration which can change rapidly, depending on the bottom where it is found. It ranges from the shallow mud and sand banks of estuaries to depths of 35 fathoms. The large toothed flounder possesses large front teeth in its upper and lower jaws. Reaches 50 cm and more than 1 kg but is most common at 30 to 35 centimetres. Flounders have a separate tail which easily distinguishes them from the sole which is another flat fish.

GARFISH, RIVER

Scientific name: Hyporhamphus regularis. Also known as Gardie, beakie, needle gar, splinter gar, lakes garfish.

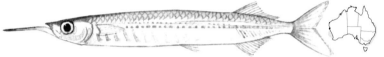

Description: The river garfish is similar in appearance to the sea garfish, but the body is slightly more stout and the silver stripe is not so prominent. The river gar also has quite large scales which are obvious when they become dislodged with handling. The beak is generally dull coloured except for the red or orange tip. The upper jaw is broader than it is long. River garfish reach 35 centimetres.

Fishing: Maggots are a particularly favoured bait in many areas. River gar are not as highly regarded as food as sea gar and need to be scaled before consumption. They are a fantastic bait for tailor, mulloway and other pelagic species.

GARFISH, SOUTHERN SEA

Scientific name: Hyporhamphus melanochir.

Description: An attractive slender fish with fine delicate scales. This species is more common in estuaries or near shore seagrass areas. The southern sea garfish reaches 50 cm and the anal fin starts below the front of the dorsal fin. The silver stripe on the side is particularly prominent.

Fishing: A common and enjoyable species to catch over or adjacent to seagrass meadows where mixed bags of Tommy rough, King George whiting and squid can be taken from the same pollard and pilchard oil berley trail. The southern sea garfish makes excellent eating.

GRENADIER

Scientific name: Macruronus novaezelandiae. Also known as Blue hake, blue grenadier, whiptail, hokl.

Description: The grenadier is a long bronze-blue fish with a distinct lateral line, the second dorsal fin is low and reaches to the end of the tapered tail where it joins the also extended anal fin. Fins are purplish-blue. Commonly found in depths of 20 to 60 m, juveniles occur in southern bays and estuaries up to tidal influences. Adults reach 1.1 metres.

Fishing: The grenadier is a common trawl species. The flesh is firm but is not as highly valued as many other species. Grenadier are taken while fishing for other species using standard bottom paternoster rigs. Grenadier readily take fish baits, squid and prawns. As with many deeper species, their fight is affected by the depth and heavier lines and sinkers commonly used.

GROPER, BALDCHIN

Scientific name: Choerodon rubescens.
Also known as Tusk-fish, baldie, bluebone.

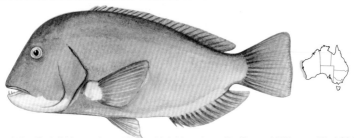

Description: The baldchin groper is one of the largest tusk-fish species reaching 90 cm and 14 kilograms. All tusk-fish have prominent protruding, tusk-like teeth in both jaws. This species is easily identified by the white chin which is more prominent in males which are larger. The pectoral fin is yellow with a pale bluish base. The tusk-fish bones have a pale bluish colour, leading to one of their common names. This species is found on inshore reefs to a depth of 40 m, with smaller fish generally found in shallower waters.

Fishing: An excellent fighting fish and one of Western Australia's premier eating fish, the baldchin groper is highly sought after. Baldchin groper are taken with standard reef fishing rigs and baits, although crabs can be particularly productive if available. Baldchin will also take prawns, octopus, squid, crabs and fish baits but there can be times when baldchin can be finicky feeders, so it pays to experiment with baits and rigs. Spearfishers can have a significant impact especially on small populations on isolated reefs.

GROPER, EASTERN BLUE

Scientific name: Achoerodus viridis. Also known as Red groper, giant pigfish, blue tank.

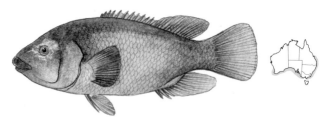

Description: The eastern blue groper can reach 20 kg but has been seriously over fished in many areas and fish of 2 to 10 kg are much more likely. The blue gropers are easily identified by their size, often brilliant colours, their fleshy lips, heavy scales and peg like teeth. The Eastern blue is found from Harvey Bay in southern Queensland to Wilson's Promontory in Victoria. Eastern blue groper prefer turbulent rocky shorelines or inshore bomboras. This species is protected from spearfishing.

Fishing: The blue groper species present a real test for shore based anglers. They can be taken on cunjevoi, prawns and squid, fresh crabs, and especially the red crabs found in the intertidal areas of the east coast. Crabs are easily the best bait. Heavy rods and line and extra strong hooks are required for these hard, dirty fighters. A groper should not be given its head as it will bury you in the nearest cave or under any rock ledge. Small to medium blue groper are good eating, but large ones are dry and the flesh coarse. These are hardy fish which many anglers choose to return to the water, as their fight is their best and most memorable feature.

Rigs and Tactics:

3 x strong

Solid brass ring

250–500 g barrel sinker

1 metre

30–50 kg trace

Dropper loop 30 cm

Main line

No. 3/0 hook - Suicide or Viking pattern

50 cm

50 cm

Dropper loop 15 cm

1/2 kg snapper sinker

GROPER, WESTERN BLUE

Scientific name: Achoerodus gouldii. Also known as giant pigfish, blue tank.

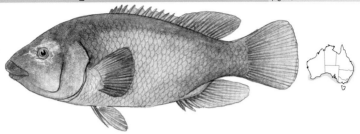

Description: The western blue groper can reach 40 kg. The blue gropers are easily identified by their size, often brilliant colours, their fleshy lips, heavy scales and peg like teeth. The Western Blue groper can be found from the Abrolhos Islands off Geraldton in Western Australia to west of Melbourne. Blue groper prefer turbulent rocky shorelines or inshore bomboras. This species is protected from spearfishing.

Fishing: The second largest wrasse species (behind the hump-headed Maori wrasse), the Western blue groper is capable of reaching 1.6 m and 40 kilograms. Blue groper present a real test for shore based anglers. They can be taken on prawns and squid, fresh crabs, and especially the rock crabs found in the intertidal areas. Heavy rods and line and extra strong hooks are required for these hard, dirty fighters. Small to medium blue groper are good eating, but large ones are dry and the flesh coarse. Some huge fish are taken on deeper reefs on the south coast of WA.

Rigs and Tactics:

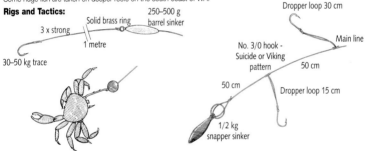

Dropper loop 30 cm

3 x strong

Solid brass ring

1 metre

250–500 g barrel sinker

30–50 kg trace

No. 3/0 hook - Suicide or Viking pattern

Main line

50 cm

50 cm

Dropper loop 15 cm

1/2 kg snapper sinker

GRUNTER, SOOTY

Scientific name: Hephaestus fuliginosus. Also known as Black bream, purple grunter, sooty.

Description: In the world, sooty grunter can reach 4kg and 50 cm, but in stocked impoundments such as Tinaroo Dam they can be considerably larger than this. This species has a reasonably large mouth and the lips may be blubbery in some specimens. Colour can be extremely variable, from light brown to black. Sooty grunter can be omnivorous and will on occasion eat green algae.

Fishing: The sooty grunter prefers faster water in rivers and can inhabit mid-stream snags in riffles. In dams these fish are found around cover, especially fallen timber. Sooty grunter will readily take live shrimp or cherabin, worms or grubs. They will readily take a variety of lures including diving lures, spinner baits, bladed spinners, jigs, soft plastics and flies. Sooty grunter fight well without jumping and are undervalued as a sport fish by many anglers, partly because they are reasonably common in many areas. Sooty grunter are a fair to poor food fish which can be weedy tasting. Species such as barramundi which occur in the same areas are much better fare.

GURNARD, RED

Scientific name: Chelidonichthys kumu. Also known as Gurnard, flying gurnard, latchet, kumu gurnard, kumukumu.

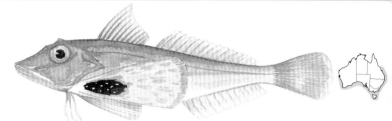

Description: The red gurnard is a beautiful species with its large pectoral fins and brightly patterned ventral fins which are bright blue with a large black spot and scattered paler spots. The first three rays of the pectoral fin are free and act as 'fingers' for the detection of food in the sand. While the head is bony, it is smooth and the red gurnard lacks the bony horns of some other species. The red gurnard can reach 60 cm and more than 2 kg but is more common at 40–45 centimetres. It is commonly found from 80 m to the continental shelf but can be taken from shallower waters at times.

Fishing: The red gurnard feeds on crabs, worms, molluscs and small fish and all these work for this species. The red gurnard is taken when fishing deeper waters for other species, being most prevalent on sand or broken ground near reefs and is generally taken on the bottom hook of a standard bottom drift rig. The fight is limited due to the depth which requires heavy lines and sinkers. The red gurnard is a highly regarded food fish.

Rigs and Tactics:

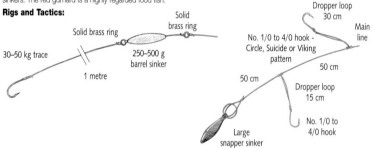

GUDGEON, FLATHEAD

Scientific name: Philypnodon grandiceps. Also known as big-headed gudgeon, freshwater gudgeon

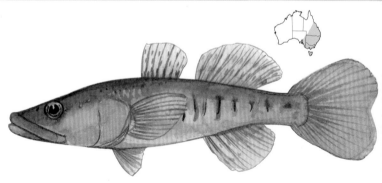

Description: A small but important forage species, the flathead gudgeon can be a common part of the diets of native fish or trout. The flathead gudgeon can reach 12 cm but is more commonly seen as 5 – 9 centimetres. The flathead gudgeon has a large head with a very large mouth for its size. There are two separate dorsal fins, which separates the gudgeons from the galaxiid minnows. The pectoral fins are large and are used to hold the fish in position. There can be a black spot at the base of the large, rounded tail fin. The colour is generally tan to chocolate brown, with a cream coloured belly. The orange eggs can be clearly seen in the belly of females as they approach breeding season.

HAIRTAIL

Scientific name: Trichiurus lepturus.
Also known as Ribbonfish, Australian hairtail, largehead hairtail, cutlassfish.

Description: The hairtail is a brilliantly silver fish which is strongly compressed and elongated, growing to 2.35 m and a weight of 6 kg, although it is frequently encountered at around 1.5 to 1.8 metres. The hairtail has fearsome fangs which also possess an anti-coagulant, making any cuts bleed profusely.

The hairtail has no tail, whereas the similar frostfish (Lepidopus caudatus) has a tiny forked tail. The hairtail has no scales, but the brilliant silver skin can be removed by rubbing with a rough cloth. They appear in some estuaries sporadically and in large numbers, but then may not be seen for several more years. The best bets for these fish are in Coal and Candle and Cowan Creeks in the Hawkesbury system and Port Kembla and Newcastle harbours during autumn and especially winter months.

Fishing: The vast majority of fish are taken at night. The hairtail is a predator which prefers live bait, with yellowtail and slimy mackerel favoured. Hairtail are often taken on dead fish such as garfish, pilchards or fresh cut flesh. Hairtail will strike lures including diving lures and vertically jigged lures or jigs when feeding well but hook-ups are difficult through the teeth. Wire traces or ganged hooks are essential and some anglers use light sticks to assist hairtail finding the bait.

As the fish are found in deep holes, setting baits at different depths until fish are found will rapidly locate the optimum depth so all baits can be moved to the same level. The hairtail is excellent to eat with delicate flesh which cooks very quickly.

Rigs and Tactics:

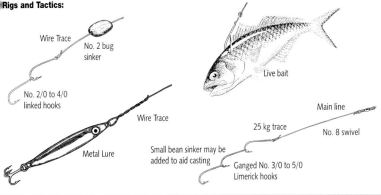

Wire Trace

No. 2 bug sinker

No. 2/0 to 4/0 linked hooks

Wire Trace

Metal Lure

Live bait

Small bean sinker may be added to aid casting

Ganged No. 3/0 to 5/0 Limerick hooks

25 kg trace

No. 8 swivel

Main line

HERRING, FRESHWATER

Scientific name: Potamalosa richmondia. Also known as Nepean herring.

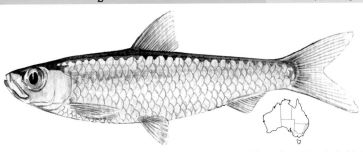

Description: The freshwater herring is an attractive silvery fish with the characteristic ventral scutes (serrations) of the true herrings. The body is slender, although some large females can develop a more robust profile. The head is scaleless and bears a superficial resemblance to the pilchard but the freshwater herring can reach 32 centimetres.

Fishing: This species is one of the best training species for fly fishers available. They are forgiving of sloppy presentation and will take dry and wet flies. The same fish will often rise repeatedly to the same fly and once hooked they are scrappy fighters who jump nicely. Freshwater herring have many fine bones but these can be consumed after the fish is cooked. Freshwater herring bruise easily and the scales can be easily dislodged so care must be taken if releasing these fish.

HARLEQUIN FISH

Scientific name: Othos dentex.
Also known as harlequin cod, Chinese lantern, tiger cod.

Description: A truly stunning species which superficially resembles the coral trout of much more tropical waters but is a bit more long and slender. The harlequin fish can have blue spots on the head of variable shape which may extend to the chin. The overall colour can vary in a similar fashion to coral trout but is more commonly red or orange and much less frequently brick red. The harlequin fish has yellow or creamy yellow blotches on the lower sides of the fish. The tail is slightly convex whereas with the coral trout species the tail is either square or concave. These species do not overlap in range but can be confused if seen together in a fish shop.

The harlequin fish inhabits coastal reefs in inshore waters. It is inquisitive and can be susceptible to spearfishing pressure. The harlequin fish can grow to 75 centimetres.

Standard reef fishing techniques rigs and baits will take harlequin fish. As they can be found in shallow reef areas, lighter sinkers and rigs work as well. The harlequin can be taken on squid, octopus, and pilchard or cut flesh baits. This species is considered very good eating.

Rigs and Tactics:

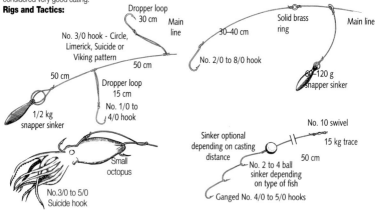

HERRING, GIANT

Scientific name: Elops machnata.
Also known as Pincushion-fish.

Description: The giant herring is a beautiful, streamlined fish covered in small scales which are easily dislodged. This species is the largest of the true herrings (Family Clupidae), reaching 1.2 m and 11 kg, although it is frequently encountered at 1 – 4 kilograms. The giant herring has a single dorsal fin with a tiny trailing last ray compared to the tarpon (page 138) which has a prominent trailing filament and a much larger eye. The giant herring has a very large upper jaw. The giant herring moves southward with warm currents and is found more commonly in summer and early autumn in more southern areas.

HERRING, AUSTRALIAN

Scientific name: Arripis georgiana. Also known as Tommy rough, tommy, ruff, bull herring, Western herring.

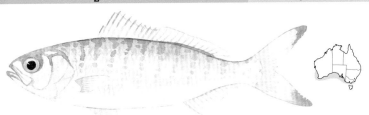

Description: A pretty and highly sought after species, the Australian herring is not a 'true' hering from the family Clupidae. Although the Australian herring can reach 40 cm, they are commonly caught at between 22 and 28 centimetres. The herring is similar to a juvenile Australian salmon, but the herring has a larger eye, black tips on the ends of the tail fin lobes and no black blotch at the base of the pectoral fin. The herring's scales feel rough when rubbed towards the head whereas an Australian salmon feels smooth which gives rise to the common name 'ruff'.

Fishing: Australian herring specialists can turn angling for these scrappy little fighters to an art form. Standard rigs include a wooden blob (float) whose hole is filled with pollard and pilchard oil, a reasonably long trace and a bait of maggot, prawn, squid or blue bait. When biting freely, Australian herring are taken on pieces of green drinking straw.

Herring are an inshore schooling fish which is commonly taken from rock groynes and beaches and are attracted to berley slicks when boat angling, especially inshore around shallow sea grass beds. Best berley includes bread, pollard, finely chopped fish scraps and chip pieces leftover from the local fish and chip shop. Herring are also taken on lures, with Halco wobblers and Tassie Devils or any small lure with red working well. On lures, herring jump as well as their cousins the salmon and although some throw the hooks, they are terrific fun. Herring are also very good eating.

Rigs and Tactics:

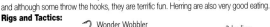

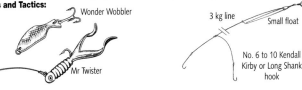

Wonder Wobbler

Mr Twister

3 kg line

Small float

Berley float

No. 6 to 10 Kendall Kirby or Long Shank hook

JAVELIN FISH, SPOTTED

Scientific name: Pomadasys kaakan. Also known as Spotted grunter-bream, grunter.

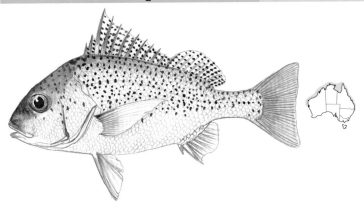

Description: The spotted javelin fish possesses black spots between the prominent spines of the dorsal fin, although these are much reduced in adult fish. The anal spine is large and prominent, giving rise to the name javelin fish. These fish grind their sharp pharyngeal (throat) teeth which is amplified by the fishes swim bladder. The spotted javelin fish is commonly found at the mouths of mangrove creeks and off rocky foreshores. They can reach 66 cm and 4.5 kilograms.

Fishing: The javelin fish feeds on prawns, crabs, worms, small fish and squid and can be taken on all these baits. The javelin fish will often run with the bait before taking it into their mouths. Therefore running sinkers and relatively light line at 4 – 6 kg is an advantage. The javelin fish can be caught on minnow lures and jigs but are rarely fished for specifically in this manner. Javelin fish are a fine table fish which can be frozen at no cost to quality.

JEWFISH, BLACK

Scientific name: Protonibea diacanthus.
Also known as Black jew, Spotted croaker, Spotted jew, Blotched jewfish, black mulloway, northern mulloway.

Description: The black mulloway is a large and prized northern mulloway species, growing to 40 kg and more than 1.5 metres. The range is important as there are few locations where black jewfish and mulloway can be taken together. The black jewfish has two prominent anal spines whereas the mulloway has a small second anal spine. The soft dorsal fin has 22 to 25 rays as opposed to 28 to 31 rays for the smaller and lighter coloured silver jewfish (Nibea soldado) of north-eastern waters which also has white ventral fins.

The black jewfish has a grey to blackish colour. Young fish have black spots on the back, dorsal and tail fins which fade in adult fish. Excellent eating.

Rigs and Tactics:

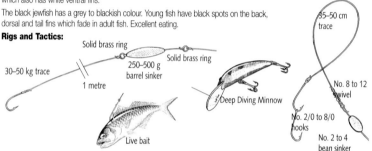

KINGFISH, YELLOWTAIL

Scientific name: Seriola lalandi. Also known as Kingie, yellowtail, hoodlum and bandit.

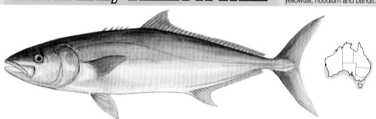

Description: The yellowtail kingfish is a beautiful, powerful fish which has a large, deeply forked tail. The back and upper sides are dark, purply blue while the lower part of the body is white. These two distinctive colours are separated by a yellow band which varies in width and intensity from fish to fish. The tail is a bright yellow. This can be a large fish reaching 2 m and more than 50 kg. Any yellowtail kingfish over 20 kg will be a memorable capture.

Fishing: The yellowtail kingfish is a brutal, dirty fighter which will fully test the skill of the angler and the quality of their gear. The first run of a kingfish is straight towards the nearest bottom obstruction to cut off an unwary angler. Kingfish will take a wide variety of lures such as minnow lures, soft plastics and flies. Vertical jigging with metal lures can be deadly. They will take a range of whole and cut fish baits, squid, octopus and cuttlefish but there are occasions when they can be finicky. At other times yellowtail kingfish will strike at bare hooks. Live bait is almost certain to attract any kingfish in the area.

Kingfish were previously considered average eating, but they have been increasingly recognised as a quality fish, including as sashimi. Large fish are worse eating and can have worms in the flesh.

Rigs and Tactics:

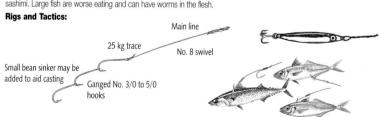

LEATHERJACKET, FAN-BELLIED

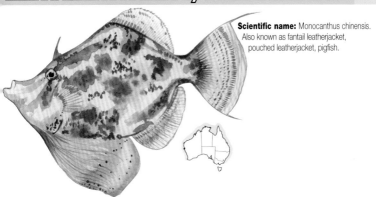

Scientific name: Monocanthus chinensis.
Also known as fantail leatherjacket,
pouched leatherjacket, pigfish.

Description: An unusual species of leatherjacket which reaches 38 centimetres. The fan-bellied leatherjacket prefers areas of seagrass or seagrass adjacent to reefs in larger estuaries and bays.

The fan-bellied leatherjacket is easily recognised by the large fan-like pouch on the abdomen. There is a large trailing filament on the top of the tail fin and there are six spines on each side of the wrist of the tail. The back rises up beyond the front spine to the dorsal fin, giving a characteristic triangular shape to the top of the fish. The colour can range from pale brown or yellow brown, through various blotched browns and to nearly black, due largely to the type of habitat in which the fish was taken.

Fishing: The fan-bellied leatherjacket is taken on a wide variety of baits and rigs. A small, long shanked hook is recommended due to the small mouth and capacity of leatherjackets to bite off light traces. Using as light a weight as possible will increase bites and hook-ups and enhance the fight of these scrappy fish. The fan-bellied leatherjacket responds to berley and can be considered a pest and a bait stealer. Larger fan-bellied leatherjackets are excellent eating. Smaller fish yield a small but tasty piece of meat when headed and skinned.

Rig and Tactics:

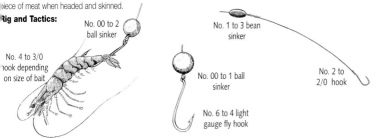

No. 00 to 2
ball sinker

No. 4 to 3/0
hook depending
on size of bait

No. 1 to 3 bean
sinker

No. 00 to 1 ball
sinker

No. 6 to 4 light
gauge fly hook

No. 2 to
2/0 hook

LEATHERJACKET, CHINAMAN

Scientific name:
Nelusetta ayraudi.

Also known as Yellow leatherjacket.

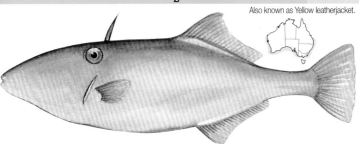

Description: The extremely long head and long first dorsal and anal rays are diagnostic of the Chinaman leatherjacket. Females and juveniles are bright orange with red-orange fins, the males yellow or yellow-brown with yellow fins. This species can be found to depths of over 350 m but juveniles school seasonally in estuaries and coastal embayments. The Chinaman leatherjacket can reach over 70 cm and 3.5 kg making it one of the world's largets leatherjackets. It is often caught in inshore waters at 25 – 35 centimetres.

LEATHERJACKET, ROUGH

Scientific name: Scobinichthys granulatus.

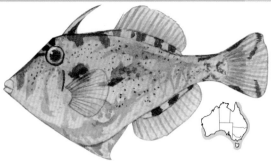

Description: This species reaches 34 cm and has no notch for the prominent dorsal spine to lay back into. The rough leather jacket has a large ventral flap, three dark lines across the forehead and dark blotchings over the back and sides. It is common in coastal seagrass beds and adjacent reefs and in estuaries.

Fishing: The rough leatherjacket will take prawns, squid, crabs, worms and cut baits. A wire trace or long shank hook can prevent bite-offs. A light line and minimal weight for the conditions can improve the fight of leatherjackets. This species is good eating.

Rig and Tactics:

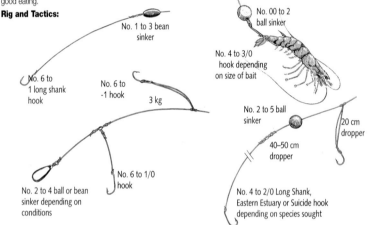

No. 1 to 3 bean sinker

No. 6 to 1 long shank hook

No. 6 to -1 hook

3 kg

No. 6 to 1/0 hook

No. 2 to 4 ball or bean sinker depending on conditions

No. 00 to 2 ball sinker

No. 4 to 3/0 hook depending on size of bait

No. 2 to 5 ball sinker

20 cm dropper

40–50 cm dropper

No. 4 to 2/0 Long Shank, Eastern Estuary or Suicide hook depending on species sought

LING, ROCK

Scientific name: Genypterus tigerinus. Also known as Tiger ling.

Description: The body of the rock ling is pale grey to white and densely patterned in black. The dorsal and anal fins lack black bars which are found on the similar pink ling. The 'beard' is actually a modified ventral fin which is positioned under the chin. Easily separated from the beardie as the rock ling does not have a tail and the dorsal and anal fins meet at the end of the body. This species can be found to depths of 60 m and adults are found on rocky reefs and broken ground while juveniles are found inshore and in bays and estuaries.

Fishing: Taken as part of mixed reef catches in cooler waters with standard reef paternoster rigs. The rock ling prefers fresh baits of cut and whole fish, squid and cuttlefish baits. This is an excellent food fish and a welcome bonus in a mixed bag.

LEATHERJACKET, SIX SPINED

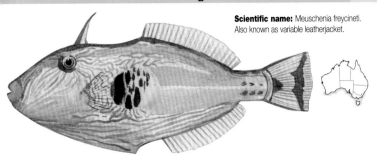

Scientific name: Meuschenia freycineti.
Also known as variable leatherjacket.

Description: The six-spined leatherjacket can reach the respectable size of 60 cm, with larger specimens found from the south coast population, although the east coast fish can be more brightly coloured. The six-spined leatherjacket is most easily identified by the prominent scribble pattern in blue or brown on the head and front part of the body. The dorsal and anal fins are yellow in the adult. The tail fin often has a black blotch at its base and a prominent black stripe, especially males. Males often have a yellow and brown blotch on their sides. Females are much less brightly coloured. There are 5 to 8 spines on each side of the wrist of the tail.

Adults are usually encountered on coastal reefs whereas juveniles, which often have prominent brown stripes along the sides and less prominent scribbling on the head, are common on seagrass meadows of estuaries and coastal bays.

Fishing: Like all leatherjackets, the six-spined leatherjacket has a small mouth and a capacity to pick larger baits intended for the larger reef fish. They show a marked preference for squid or prawn baits but can be taken on a wide variety of baits. A fairly small, long shanked hook is recommended and some anglers use a light wire trace to avoid bite-offs. The difficulty in hooking leatherjackets is more than offset by their excellent eating qualities. They can be headed and the skin peeled off by hand for a very high quality meal.

Rigs and Tactics:

No. 4 to 2/0 hook

No. 2 to 4 ball or bean sinker depending on conditions

3 kg

No. 4 to 2/0 hook

No. 00 to 2 ball sinker

No. 4 to 1 Suicide or baitholder hook

No. 8 to 12 long shank hook

Small split shot

Small slices of fish bait

LONGTOM, SLENDER

Scientific name: Stronylura leiura.
Also known as common longtom

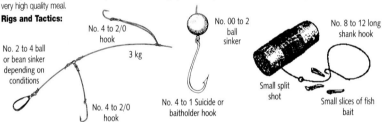

Description: The common name is quite apt as the slender longtom is a slender and sleek species. The slender longtom is most easily separated from other longtoms by the bar along the base of the gill cover which can fade after death. The tail fin is square or may be convex. The jaws are elongated and fine and filled with needle sharp teeth.

The slender longtom is most commonly found in coastal waters and can be found in large bays and estuaries. This species can reach 110 cm but is most frequently encountered in estuaries at a smaller size.

LUDERICK

Scientific name: Girella tricuspidata.
Also known as Blackfish, darkie, bronzie.

Description: The luderick has up to 12 narrow vertical dark bars on its upper body. The colour varies from almost black to a pale purplish colour depending on the wash in the area of capture. The tail fin is darker than the body.

Luderick are a schooling species, although the largest specimens form much smaller groups. Luderick can reach more than 2 kg but are more common at 500–900 grams.

Fishing: While some quality luderick angling can be had in estuaries, it is fishing from ocean rocks that provides the greatest challenge. A long, soft action rod is most important to quickly pick up slack line during swells and when setting the hook, to cushion the fight of the fish and to assist in washing the fish up when landing it. A centrepin reel is favoured so that line can be paid out quickly during the drift. The most effective rig is a well-balanced float rig. As a rule, the lower the swell, the deeper you fish; up to 3 m or so. A light trace (around 3 kg) is important when using a sliding float rig, to prevent the loss of the float to snags or broken-off fish. All but the tip of the float should be under the water while fishing. Allow the float to fully disappear below the surface before taking up the slack line on a smooth strike action.

The two most common baits are string or ribbon weed or cabbage (Ulva latuca). Use some for berley, either trickled into the water or chopped and mixed with sand. Berley is very important as it attracts nearby schools of luderick. With cabbage, the best bait is a small tight rosette, with the hook inserted through the nodule at the base. A small, tidy bright green bait works best. Wind string weed around the hook so that it puffs out nicely in the water.

Work the water close in first, as luderick can be virtually under your feet. Luderick are rarely taken very far past the edge of the turbulent water in the wash zone. They should be bled as soon as possible.

Rigs and Tactics:

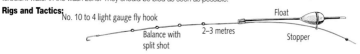

No. 10 to 4 light gauge fly hook
Balance with split shot
2–3 metres
Float
Stopper

LUNGFISH

Scientific name: Girella tricuspidata.
Also known as Blackfish, darkie, bronzie, nigger.

Description: The Australian lungfish is the most primitive of Australia's freshwater fish, which has remained unchanged for over 100 million years. The head is large and the eye very small. The body is brown and covered in large scales. The pectoral fins are large and paddle-like as are the well set back pelvic fins. The tail is extremely fleshy and though broad, is eel-like. The Australian lungfish possesses a single lung and can gulp air from the surface of oxygen poor waters, but unlike the African and American lungfish, it cannot survive completely out of water for extended periods.

Fishing: The lungfish is omnivorous, eating weed on occasion and can be accidentally taken on worms, frogs or shrimp. They are sluggish fighters and as they are totally protected, should be immediately returned to the water.

MACKEREL, FRIGATE

Scientific name: Auxis thazard.
Also known as Little tuna.

Description: A handsome fish which can reach 60 cm and around 5 kilograms. The frigate mackerel possesses the distinctive broken oblique lines above the lateral line and no markings below the lateral line. It can be easily separated from the similar mackerel tuna as the frigate mackerel has a wide gap between the two dorsal fins, no black spots near the ventral fins and a more slender body. The frigate mackerel can form large shoals in coastal or inshore waters.

Fishing: The frigate mackerel will readily take quickly trolled silver or chrome lures. Christmas tree type lures work well trolled in a pattern. High speed spinning can work well. This species can be finicky at times, with large schools refusing all offerings, but on other occasions will strike savagely at any lure and will take trolled or cast dead baits. The frigate mackerel fights well for its size. It makes terrific bait, either trolled for billfish, or as cut bait for reef species. The frigate mackerel is not highly regarded as a food fish, but is suitable for sashimi or for poaching.

MACKEREL, QUEENSLAND SCHOOL

Scientific name: Scomberomorus queenslandicus.
Also known as school mackerel, doggie mackerel, blotched mackerel, shiny mackerel.

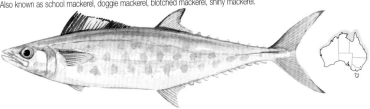

Description: The Queensland school mackerel is a schooling species which frequents inshore areas. The Queensland school mackerel can reach a metre in length and a weight of 12 kilograms. However they are commonly encountered from 1.5 to 4 kg, especially on the eastern seaboard. This species is easily identified by the large dark spots on the sides and the black then white areas on the first dorsal fin. The pectoral fin is also smaller and more pointed than in the broad-barred Spanish mackerel.

Fishing: Schools of Queensland school mackerel can be berleyed close to the boat and taken with live or whole dead or fresh cut bait. These fish will take lures but can be finicky. Queensland school mackerel can patrol close to the shore and can be a surprise catch from tropical beaches or creek mouths, but they can bite off lures or baits intended for other species. The Queensland school mackerel is a top table fish if filleted.

Rigs and Tactics:

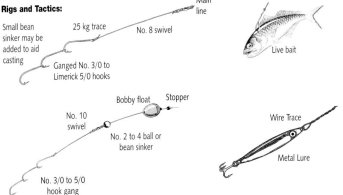

Main line

Small bean sinker may be added to aid casting

25 kg trace

No. 8 swivel

Ganged No. 3/0 to Limerick 5/0 hooks

Live bait

Bobby float

Stopper

No. 10 swivel

No. 2 to 4 ball or bean sinker

No. 3/0 to 5/0 hook gang

Wire Trace

Metal Lure

MACKERAL, SLIMY

Scientific name: Scomber australasicus. Also known as Blue mackerel, spotted chub mackerel, slimies.

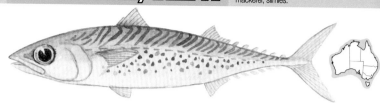

Description: A relatively small species, reaching 65 cm and 2 kg but which is most often encountered at 25 – 35 centimetres. The slimy mackerel has wavy bars on its back, spots on its side and 5 – 6 finlets behind both the dorsal and anal fins. It can be separated from the jack or horse mackerel as it lacks the bony scutes along the rear of the lateral line. Slimy mackerel travel in schools which can enter bays and some larger estuaries. The slimy mackerel is an extremely important forage species with many pelagic species attracted to feed on slimies. The decimation of pilchard stocks by virus has made slimies even more important. Proposals to increase commercial slimy mackerel exploitation has angered recreational fishers as the impact on local fishing quality is likely to be severe.

Fishing: The slimy mackerel is often taken for granted, taken in quantity for live bait with the use of bait jigs on recognised bait grounds. Slimy mackerel is also a first class cut bait as the oily flesh is attractive to many species. Slimy mackerel react well to berley and in many areas great fun can be had on slimies mixed with Australian herring, garfish and tailor or juvenile Australian salmon. The slimy mackerel is not highly regarded as food as it has a strong fishy taste, but they are popular in some Mediterranean cooking which values the stronger fish flavour.

MACKERAL, BROAD-BARRED SPANISH

Scientific name: Scomberomorus semifasciatus. Also known as Grey mackerel, tiger mackerel, broad barred mackerel.

Description: A similar species to the more common and generally larger Spanish mackerel, they can be readily identified by the much larger soft dorsal and anal fins. The bars are much broader and fewer in number with live fish, but they fade significantly on death, giving rise to the marketing name of grey mackerel. The broad-barred Spanish mackerel reaches 1.2 m and 8 kg but is commonly caught at 1 – 3 kg from inshore waters or major embayments such as Tin Can Bay in Queensland.

Fishing: Like its larger cousin, the broad-barred Spanish mackerel readily takes small minnow or chrome lures and whole or cut fish baits. Live baits work extremely well. This species fights well, particularly on light line but is not as highly regarded a food fish as the Spanish mackerel.

Rigs and Tactics:

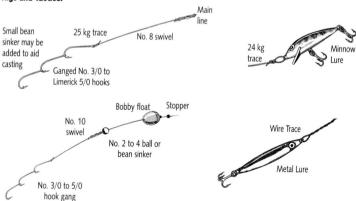

MACKEREL, FRIGATE

Scientific name: Auxis thazard.
Also known as Little tuna.

Description: A handsome fish which can reach 60 cm and around 5 kilograms. The frigate mackerel possesses the distinctive broken oblique lines above the lateral line and no markings below the lateral line. It can be easily separated from the similar mackerel tuna as the frigate mackerel has a wide gap between the two dorsal fins, no black spots near the ventral fins and a more slender body. The frigate mackerel can form large shoals in coastal or inshore waters.

Rigs and Tactics:

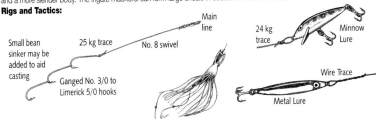

Small bean sinker may be added to aid casting

25 kg trace

Ganged No. 3/0 to Limerick 5/0 hooks

No. 8 swivel

Main line

24 kg trace

Minnow Lure

Wire Trace

Metal Lure

MACKEREL, SHARK

Scientific name: Grammatorcynus bicarinatus.
Also known as Scaly mackerel, large-scaled tunny, salmon mackerel.

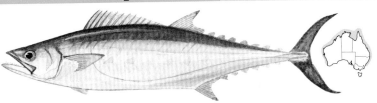

Description: A sought after fish found on shallow reef areas throughout its range. This species has a distinguishing double lateral line which divides at the pectoral fin and joins again at the tail base. The belly displays dark spots and the eye is relatively small, especially compared to the similar double lined (or scad) mackerel. The scales of the shark mackerel come away in large sheets.

The name shark mackerel comes from a distinctive ammonia smell (shark-like) when the fish is cleaned but which disappears with cooking. The shark mackerel can reach 1.3 m and 11 kilograms.

Fishing: Shark mackerel are good lure prospects, rising to take minnow or spoon type lure where they put up a determined surface based fight. Shark mackerel are also taken on drifted whole or cut fish baits and live baits, although shark mackerel are not the general target species with live baits in tropical waters. The shark mackerel makes reasonable eating but the quality is improved by skinning the fillets.

Rigs and Tactics:

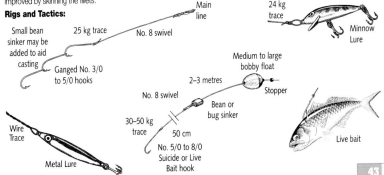

Small bean sinker may be added to aid casting

25 kg trace

Ganged No. 3/0 to 5/0 hooks

No. 8 swivel

Main line

24 kg trace

Minnow Lure

Medium to large bobby float

2–3 metres

Stopper

No. 8 swivel

Bean or bug sinker

30–50 kg trace

50 cm

No. 5/0 to 8/0 Suicide or Live Bait hook

Wire Trace

Metal Lure

Live bait

MACKEREL, SPANISH

Scientific name:
Scomberomorus commerson.

Also known as Narrow-barred Spanish mackerel, blue mackerel,
tanguigue, Spaniard, seer, seerfish.

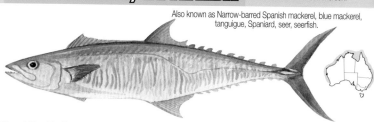

Description: The Spanish mackerel is a highly sought after and valued species capable of reaching 2.35 m and 42 kilograms. It is commonly taken from 5 – 15 kilograms. Smaller fish travel in pods of similar sized fish. The Spanish mackerel is similar to the wahoo but has fewer dorsal spines (15 – 18 versus 23 – 27) in a shorter dorsal fin. The upper jaw of the Spanish mackerel has an obvious external bone which extends to at least the middle of the eye, while in the wahoo there is no obvious bone and the upper jaw extends to the front edge of the eye. The Spanish mackerel is found in coastal waters, frequently in the vicinity of reefs.

Fishing: Spanish mackerel will aggressively take trolled lures and baits. Minnow lures, spoons and feathered lures run at 5 – 7 knots work best, while trolled garfish, slimy mackerel or other fish at 3 – 5 knots will take good catches. Spanish mackerel will also take drifted live, whole or cut baits. Land based fishermen drift large baits under balloons to take large fish. A wire trace is an effective counter to the sharp teeth.

The Spanish mackerel is an excellent sport fish, particularly on light line, as it runs strongly and occasionally jumps in its attempts to escape. Spanish mackerel can actively feed at different depths,

so lures and baits which target a wide range will more quickly locate fish.It is a highly regarded food fish, but does not freeze particularly well. The quality is much better when the fish is filleted.

Rigs and tactics:

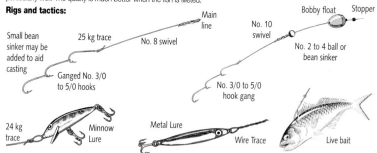

Small bean sinker may be added to aid casting

25 kg trace

No. 8 swivel

Main line

No. 10 swivel

Bobby float   Stopper

No. 2 to 4 ball or bean sinker

Ganged No. 3/0 to 5/0 hooks

No. 3/0 to 5/0 hook gang

24 kg trace

Minnow Lure

Metal Lure

Wire Trace

Live bait

MARLIN, BLACK

Scientific name: Makaira indica.
Also known as Giant black marlin, silver marlin.

Description: A magnificent blue water billfish capable of reaching a length of nearly 5 m and 850 kilograms. The black marlin is readily distinguished by its rigid pectoral fins which cannot be laid next to body in any black marlin and are completely rigid in all fish over 50 kg. In this fairly heavy bodied fish, the start of the second dorsal is forward to the start of the second anal fin. Black marlin are most commonly found in blue water, with fish moving southwards as far as Augusta with the warmer currents. Black marlin are found above deep structure along current lines and where baitfish aggregations are prevalent.

MARLIN, STRIPED

Scientific name: Tetrapturus audax.
Also known as Striper, stripey.

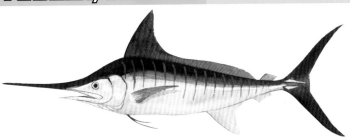

Description: The striped marlin is more compressed than the other more cylindrical marlin species. The striped marlin reaches a smaller maximum size than the black and blue marlin at 250 kg, with Australian specimens encountered to over 150 kilograms.

The striped marlin has striking cobalt blue or lavender stripes which fade to a fair degree after death. The first three rays in the high first dorsal are of similar height. The striped marlin also has a single lateral line which may not be readily visible but which is raised and can be felt. The pectoral fin is longer than the body depth and can fold against the body. The tail appears squared off at the end of the top and bottom lobe.

MAHI MAHI

Scientific name: Coryphaena hippurus.
Also known as Dolphin, dolphin fish, common dolphinfish, dorado.

Description: The mahi mahi is one of the most beautiful fish in the ocean when lit up, with bright yellow to blue colouration and brilliant blue flecks over most of the body and fins. The fantastic colours fade to a washed out grey after death. Mature male or 'bull' mahi mahi have a prominent high forehead and tend to be more brightly coloured. Females have a more streamlined head profile.

The species is easily recognised in photographs due to its shape and brilliant colours. Other diagnostic features include the very long dorsal and anal fins and the deeply veed tail.

Mahi mahi are arguably the fastest growing species in the ocean, growing as much as a centimetre a day when food is plentiful. Mahi mahi can reach 2 m and more than 20 kg but are frequently taken in Australia from 2 to 10 kilograms. In Western Australia, mahi mahi are first found in oceanic waters at less than a kilogram and within five months, those that have not been caught are more than 10 kilograms.

Rigs and Tactics:

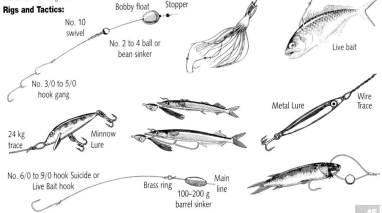

MANGROVE JACK

Scientific name: Lutjanus argentimaculatus.
Also known as Jacks, red bream, dog bream, red perch, reef red bream, purple sea perch, creek red bream.

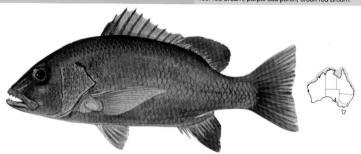

Description: The mangrove jack is best known for its destruction of fishing tackle in tidal creeks, but these tend to be juvenile or small adult fish. The largest specimens are taken on offshore reefs to a depth of 100 metres. Mangrove jack can reach more than 1.2 m and a weight of 15 kg but fish in inshore waters are a real handful at 1 – 3 kilograms.

The mangrove jack is often confused with the red bass, which is a much more notorious ciguatera species, especially if caught on reefs. The mangrove jack has a taller dorsal fin, a lack of lengthwise stripes on its side and the absence of black on the fins. Mangrove jacks lack the distinctive pit before the eye of the red bass which is predominantly a coral reef species.

Rigs and Tactics:

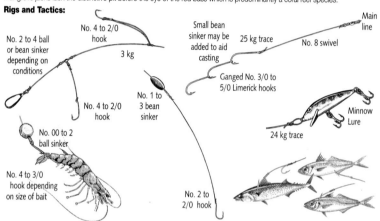

MARRON

Scientific name: Cherax. Also known as Freshwater crayfish.

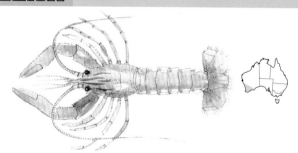

Description: The marron is a large freshwater crustacean, reaching nearly 2 kg and a total length of over 38 centimetres. Marron can be identified by the fairly light claws and the five distinct keels on the head and two spines on the tail fan. Marron are generally a dark brown, although large marron that moult less frequently can have quite dirty shells. Marron can be separated from the other native Western Australian crustaceans. Koonacs have heavier claws and more closely resemble yabbies but have four less obvious head keels. Gilgies have heavier claws than marron and lack the serrations on the outside of the claws. Gilgies only grow to 12 cm and have a mottled colour.

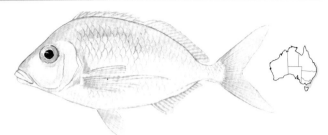

MORWONG

Scientific name: Nemadactylus douglasii.
Also known as Grey morwong, silver morwong, blue morwong, common morwong, rubberlip, blubberlip, jackass, mowie, sea bream, porae (NZ).

Description: The morwong is a deep bodied fish with a relatively small mouth and prominent fleshy lips. The colour ranges from a pale grey to silver and to silvery blue. In common with other morwong, this species has several extended rays in each pectoral fin. Morwong can reach 70 cm and more than 4 kg, but is commonly caught at 1–2 kilograms. The morwong can be separated from the banded morwong and red morwong by their distinctive colourations and the queen snapper has distinctive gold lines on the head in large adults and gold stripes on smaller fish.

Fishing: The morwong was once considered a poor second alternative to snapper, particularly in NSW, but increasingly scarce snapper numbers have elevated morwong to a more desirable species.

Morwong feed on prawns, worms, squid, molluscs, fish flesh and other food which they encounter opportunistically. Best baits include fish flesh, prawns, squid and octopus tentacles. Baits are presented on a traditional two hook paternoster rig, with sufficient weight to reach the bottom and bounce along on a slow drift. Morwong are often found in small loose schools so once fish are encountered, repeated drifts over the same area should continue to produce fish. If the current or wind is strong, a drogue or drift anchor will slow the drift and keep the baits in productive water which includes the edges of deep water reefs and drop-offs, with broken rock and gravel being particularly important. On occasions morwong can be taken over sand or mud bottoms, but a depth sounder is important to save time as fish feed more infrequently in these areas.

Morwong are most commonly encountered from 30 to 200 m, but they are occasionally taken from shallower waters. They are an easy target for spearfishermen. The morwong is fair to good eating but can have a slight iodine taste, especially if fish have been grazing on weed which they occasionally do. Filleting helps improve the quality of the flesh.

Rigs and Tactics:

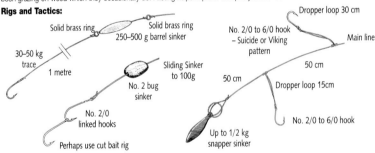

MOSQUITO FISH

Scientific name: Gambusia affinis. Also known as Gambusia, eastern gambusia, gambies, Starling's perch.

Description: The mosquito fish is a small species, females reach 6 cm with males no larger than 3.5 centimetres. The mosquito fish is a live bearer, giving birth to miniature live young. The mosquito fish is a less colourful and flamboyant relative of the common guppy. The larger female has a prominent black spot at the rear of the abdomen where the young develop. The males have a large and prominent first anal ray which is called a gonopodium and is used to internally fertilise the eggs within the female. Under good conditions young mosquito fish can reach maturity within two months. Mosquito fish can rapidly build up populations, leading to large schools of these voracious fish which regrettably prefer foods other than mosquito larvae when alternatives are available.

MOUTH ALMIGHTY

Scientific name: Glossamia aprion. Also known as Northern mouthbreeder, gobbleguts.

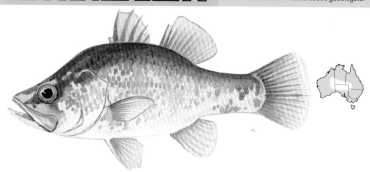

Description: An aggressive and very game species, the mouth almighty will try to eat any live food which is smaller than it is. The mouth almighty can reach 20 cm and 600 g but is commonly much smaller than that size. The mouth almighty has a pointed snout and a large mouth which extends behind the very large eye. A dark bar extends from the shoulder through the eye. The base colour may vary but is a shade of brown and can change rapidly when the fish is frightened. The mouth almighty is a mouth brooder, with the male taking up the eggs and holding them until they hatch.

Fishing: The mouth almighty is a solitary animal which prefers still, weedy areas and as a result is not often encountered by anglers. They can be taken on worms, live shrimp and small live fish. Mouth almighty are occasionally taken on lures. Mouth almighty make an interesting aquarium fish but don't readily take dead food and will consume or harass other fish.

MULLET, YELLOW-EYE

Scientific name: Aldrichetta forsteri. Also known as Pilch or pilchard, estuary mullet, freshwater mullet, yelloweye.

Description: A very common species of southern estuaries and embayments. Yellow-eye mullet also move on or just off beaches near estuaries during winter in Western Australia. The bright yellow eye, without the gelatinous eye covering, is diagnostic. This species also has small teeth in both jaws and 12 rays in the anal fin. The yellow-eye mullet grows to 50 cm and more than 1 kg, but is most common at around 30 centimetres.

Fishing: In Western Australia, yellow-eye mullet are much more aggressive feeders and will take a much wider variety of baits, although they can be quite finicky, especially deep within estuaries. During winter on beaches or the mouths of estuaries, yellow-eye mullet readily take blue bait or whitebait as well as prawn, pipi, worms, maggots or small pieces of squid. Berley improves catches. Standard light surf rigs or double hook estuarine rigs works well. Yellow-eye mullet are often very close to shore, so long casts are not always necessary and the cast should be fished right to the shore. Yellow-eye mullet are good eating, especially fish which are taken from beaches or have not been grazing on algae.

Rigs and Tactics:

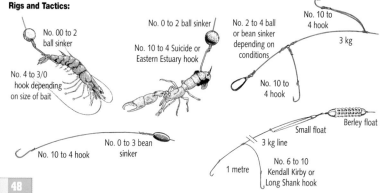

MULLET, SAND

Scientific name: Myxus elongatus.
Also known as Tallegalane, black spot mullet, lano.

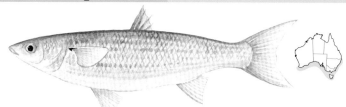

Description: The sand mullet is a moderately small mullet reaching 41 cm and nudging a kilogram but most commonly encountered around 25–30 centimetres.

This species has a straight upper profile and pointed head which differs from the sea mullet which has a more rounded snout. The sand mullet generally has a black blotch at the top of the base of the pectoral fin. The sand mullet lacks the obvious fatty eyelid of the sea mullet and several other species. The eye colour is yellow-brown or light brown as opposed to the bright yellow of the yellow-eye mullet, but the most obvious difference is that the sand mullet has 9 rays in the anal fin and the yellow-eye mullet 12 rays. The sand mullet is found in bays, lower estuaries and ocean beaches in schools, usually of similar sized fish. They have a strong preference for sandy bottoms but can be found over mud or weed bottoms on occasions.

Fishing: The sand mullet is frequently taken on baits. It will take bread and is particularly susceptible if berleyed up with bread and fished near the surface with a small pinch of dough or bread which is squeezed on the hook. Sand mullet will also take prawns, beach and blood worms, nippers, maggots and occasionally small pieces of skinned squid or octopus.

The sand mullet will rise to baits so small float rigs work well. A good trick in tidal areas is to use a small float of quill or even cork held against the current with small split shot to a size 12 long shank hook with the bread or dough bait. In estuaries, keep the bait in the finely ground berley trail and allow the fish to hook themselves against the current. Where there is a sandy bottom, very light bottom rigs can produce good mixed bags of mullet, whiting, bream, trevally and flathead. Small prawn pieces can improve your scope for other species, but a smaller hook is recommended for sand mullet. Keeping the bait moving attracts bites and helps to work out when a bread bait may have washed off the hook.

Sand mullet are good eating and their slightly oily flesh is ideal for nearly every fish recipe. Mullet also make ideal live, dead or cut bait.

Rigs and Tactics:

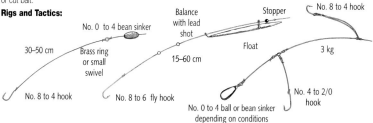

MULLET, SEA

Scientific name: Mugil cephalus.
Also known as Bully mullet, bully, mullet, hard-gut mullet, river mullet. Juveniles referred to as poddy mullet or poddies.

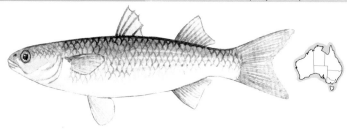

Description: The sea mullet is a cylindrical barrel of muscle which is readily identified by the thick, transparent, gelatinous covering over all but the centre of the eyes. They often have several diffuse lateral stripes on the side, but the colour and intensity can vary with the environment. Sea mullet have a distinguishing enlarged and pointed scale behind the top of the pectoral fin.

Sea mullet are found from far above the tidal reaches of coastal rivers to reasonable distances offshore, but they are best known for the vast shoals they can form at spawning time on east coast beaches. They are a very large species, reaching 80 cm and over 5 kg, but sea mullet are most commonly encountered at 1–2 kilograms. They fight extremely hard when enticed with bread, burley and bait.

MULLOWAY

Scientific name: Argyrosomus japonicus.
Also known as Jewfish, jew, jewie, butterfish, river kingfish, silver kingfish.

Small fish to around 3 kg are generally referred to as soapies due to their rather bland or soapy taste. Fish from 3–8 kg are frequently known as Schoolies as they are often encountered in schools which decrease in number as the size increases.

Description: Mulloway are a large and highly prized species found in estuaries, embayments and inshore ocean waters throughout its range. The mulloway can vary in colour from dark bronze to silver and there may be red or purple tinges, but a silver ocean mulloway is a stunning fish.

The mulloway has large scales and a generous mouth. A line of silvery spots follows the lateral line in live fish which glows under artificial lights as do the eyes which shine a bright red. A conspicuous black spot is just above the pectoral fin. The tail fin is convex (rounded outwards).

Mulloway can reach 1.8 m and more than 60 kg, but any fish over 25 kg is worth long term boasting rights for the angler.

Rigs and Tactics:

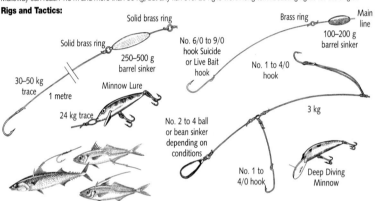

MORWONG, RED

Scientific name: Cheilodactylus fuscus.
Also known as Five-fingers.

Description: The red morwong possesses the typical extended lower rays of the pectoral fin and the prominent rubbery lips. This species is more common on inshore reefs or off rocky headlands. There is a distinctive red colouration on the upper body with several prominent white splotches and white bars near the tail. A red stripe runs through the eye. The red morwong reaches 45 cm and 3 kg but is more common around 1 kilogram.

NANNYGAI

Scientific name: Centroberyx affinis.
Also known as Eastern nannygai, redfish.

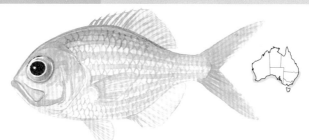

Description: A pink to bright red or orange coloured fish, with large eyes, a large upturned mouth, a rounded snout and no pale fin margins. The nannygai is separated from other similar species such as the red snapper as it has 7 as opposed to 6 dorsal spines.

While juveniles can school in estuaries and on inshore reefs, larger fish are found in larger schools in waters deeper than 25 m and out towards the edge of the continental shelf where they are a common trawl species. The nannygai is not a large fish, reaching around 45 centimetres.

Fishing: The nannygai is often encountered when fishing deeper reefs for snapper and other deep water species. The large weights and relatively small size of nannygai means that they are less highly regarded than many other species. The large mouth and schooling nature of the nannygai means that large numbers can be caught, and on large baits.

Standard snapper paternoster rigs with sufficient weight to drag bottom on a drift will take nannygai. Nannygai can be found near offshore reefs or near drop-offs over gravel or silt bottoms. Nannygai will take baits of fish, squid, octopus, crab, prawn and pilchard. When nannygai are biting freely, a fish can be caught on each hook on each drop and will often beat any snapper or other target species to the hook. Nannygai make good eating with firm white fillets. They are taken by trawlers in large quantities and are marketed as redfish.

Rigs and Tactics:

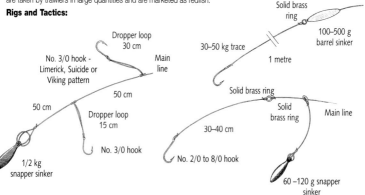

PARROTFISH

Scientific name: Family Scaridae.

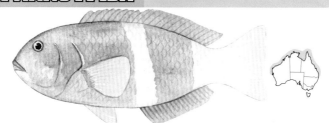

Description: Closely related to the similarly colourful wrasses, but parrotfish have their teeth fused into strong beak-like plates. Sexes can have different colours and juveniles often have very different colours from adults. Some parrotfish can change sex when the largest male in a group is removed. Many parrotfish sleep in reef caves at night and can secrete a mucous envelope around their bodies while they rest. Sizes of parrotfish can range from the humphead parrotfish which can be up to 1.2 m to the more common green finned parrotfish which reaches 30 centimetres.

PERCH, MOSES

Scientific name: Lutjanus russelli.
Also known as One spot sea perch, fingermark (WA).

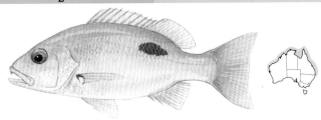

Description: Has a general reddish or pinkish hue, a large mouth with discernible canine teeth and 14 or 15 rays in the dorsal fin. The Moses perch has a distinctive black spot which can be quite pale, below the start of the soft dorsal rays. Most of the black spot is above the obvious lateral line, while the similar black-spot sea perch (Lutjanus fulviflamma) has a small black spot, most of which is below the lateral line. The lateral yellow stripes of the black-spot sea perch are not present on the Moses perch.

The Moses perch often forms schools of similar sized fish, hanging near coral outcrops and in eddies near reefs. They can be found near drop-offs, on reefs or in depths of up to 80 m, with larger specimens frequently captured from deeper water. The Moses perch reaches 50 cm and nearly 3 kg but is commonly caught at between 25 and 30 centimetres.

Fishing: Like many species in this group, the Moses perch can be an aggressive feeder, rising well to minnow lures, feather jigs and even surface poppers cast or trolled to the downstream side of coral outcrops. The school can jostle to be the first to take the lure or bait.

Baits include whole or cut fish baits, squid, octopus or prawns. Weights should be kept to a minimum depending on the depth and mood of the fish, as Moses perch will rise to a bait which also puts them further from dangerous coral which they will try to use. In deeper water, lighter weights allow the fish to fight better and keeping the bait just above the bottom will deter some pickers .

The Moses perch is a good eating fish.

Rigs and Tactics:

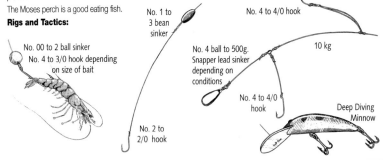

No. 1 to 3 bean sinker

No. 00 to 2 ball sinker
No. 4 to 3/0 hook depending on size of bait

No. 4 ball to 500g. Snapper lead sinker depending on conditions

No. 4 to 4/0 hook

10 kg

No. 4 to 4/0 hook

Deep Diving Minnow

No. 2 to 2/0 hook

PERCH, PEARL

Scientific name: Glaucosoma scapulare.
Also known as Pearly, nannygai (QLD).

Description: This is a handsome fish with a large eye and a large mouth. There is a small black spot at the base of the pectoral fin and a distinctive black flap of skin and bone near the top back edge of the gill cover. The pearl perch can reach 5 kg, but a fish over 3 kg is a quality fish.

Fishing: This is widely regarded as one of the best, if not the best eating fish on the east coast. It was once found on mid depth reefs as far south as Newcastle, but commercial and recreational overfishing has pushed these fish further north and onto less heavily fished deep reefs in more than 50 m of water.

PERCH, SILVER

Scientific name: Bidyanus bidyanus.
Also known as grunter, black bream, bidyan, Murray perch, tcheri, freshwater bream, silver.

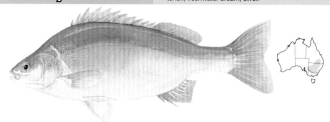

Description: The silver perch is a fine freshwater fish species, reaching 8 kg but most frequently encountered at between 0.3 kg and 1 kg, especially in impoundments. Larger silver perch frequently become omnivorous or almost entirely vegetarian, full of the green slimy weed which can seriously affect lure and bait fishing at some times of the year.

The silver perch has a small head and small mouth, but they take large lures on occasions. As the fish grows, its head appears smaller than its body, especially in dams where fast growth rates leave a heavier body in larger fish. The rear margin of the small scales is dark grey or deep brown which gives a cross hatched appearance. The fish may grunt on capture but this is not as loud or as common as in other species. In dams especially, silver perch form schools of similar sized fish, with smaller schools of large fish.

Fishing: Silver perch are becoming increasingly rare in rivers. In NSW silver perch may only be taken from stocked impoundments. Quite easy to breed in hatcheries, large numbers have been stocked into dams throughout south-eastern Australia. In rivers, Silver perch prefer faster water and can be taken in or downstream of rapids or broken water. Best baits are worms, peeled yabby tail, shrimps and a variety of smaller grubs. More exotic baits like snails, ox heart and chicken breast will also take fish on occasion. Silver perch can sometimes be found schooled near sunken timber where bobbing with worm or small yabby baits will pick up silvers and other species. Silver perch will take lures, but their small mouth means that small lures are best. In rivers or shallow waters silver perch love Celta or other spinner type lures, while small minnows like the Mann's 5+, McGrath minnow, small Legend Lure and small Halco Laser lures work well.

Silver perch fight well and are a good eating fish, although larger specimens can be dry and may have a slight weed taint.

Rigs and Tactics:

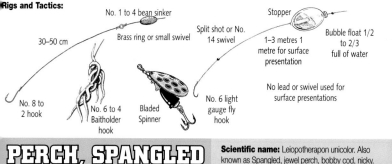

PERCH, SPANGLED

Scientific name: Leiopotherapon unicolor. Also known as Spangled, jewel perch, bobby cod, nicky.

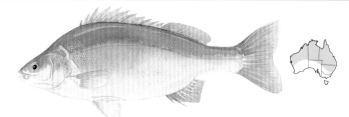

Description: The spangled perch is a small, aggressive schooling fish with characteristic pattern of rusty or golden brown spots over a generally brown or silvery body. The spangled perch can reach 600 g, but in some waters, hordes of fish of 50 – 200 g will consume any baits in the vicinity.

Fishing: They will take baits of worms, grubs, maggots, shrimps, small yabbies, peeled yabby tail and small fish. Spangled perch will also take small lures such as micro jigs. Their fairly large mouth and strong appetite means that they can take baits intended for larger fish. Where legal, spangled perch make a hardy live bait for other species.

PIKE, LONGFINNED

Scientific name: Dinolestes lewini.
Also known as Pike, jack pike, skipjack pike.

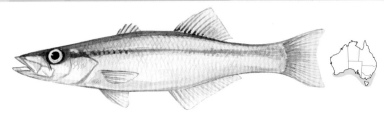

Description: The longfinned pike is a long slender fish with a large head, large mouth and an underslung jaw extending almost to the front edge of the large eye. This species has two distinct dorsal fins. A prominent and extended anal fin separates this species from the similar striped seapike which also has 2–3 brown lateral stripes along its side. The tail and wrist of the tail of the long finned pike are yellow or golden whereas in the striped seapike the tail has a yellow hue, especially near the back edge. The longfinned pike can be confused with the snook, which has the two dorsal fins widely separated and the ventral fin is set well behind the pectoral fin. The snook is a much larger species, reaching more than a metre and over 5 kilograms.

The longfinned pike can reach more than 2 kg and 90 cm but is most often encountered at between 40 and 50 centimetres. It takes chrome lures and dead and live baits well.

QUEENFISH

Scientific name: Scomberoides commersonnianus. Also known as Giant leatherskin, leatherskin, queenie, talang queenfish, skinny, skinnyfish.

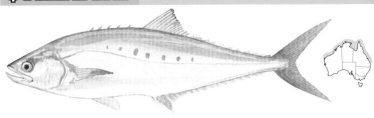

Description: The queenfish is a large, long and laterally (side to side) compressed species which leads to the common name of skinny and a light weight for the length. The mouth is large and extends mouth well beyond the back of the eye whereas other smaller queenfish species have smaller mouths. A series of 5 to 8 oval shaped blotches are found on the sides above the lateral line. The similar but smaller double spotted queenfish (Scomberoides lysan) has a double row of spots above and below the lateral line. The queenfish also has a prominent, high and light coloured front part of the dorsal and anal fins. These fish have lance shaped scales which are deeply embedded in a leathery skin. The queenfish can reach 120 cm and more than 11 kilograms. This light weight for the length indicates how skinny the queenfish is when viewed head on.

Fishing: Queenfish are found from the upper tidal reaches of tropical rivers to inshore reefs and occasionally near outer reefs which have shallow breaks. Queenfish prefer slightly turbid water with plenty of flow. They are ambush feeders and will lurk near cover such as eddies, rock bars, wharves and creek mouths, especially on a falling tide.

Queenfish are spectacular and exciting sportfish, with their slashing strikes and blistering runs, often with aerial displays. Queenfish will take dead baits such as mullet, pilchard, garfish, mudskippers, whiting or fresh prawns and squid. They are partial to live bait. Queenfish are renowned lure takers, with cast or trolled lures such as sliced chrome lures, spoons, shallow and deep diving minnows, and surface lures. Queenfish are excited by escaping baitfish, so a fast, erratic retrieve is most successful.

Fly enthusiasts are increasingly targeting queenfish. Large minnow type flies retrieved through current eddies on a fast strip works best. A heavy monofilament leader is recommended when fishing for queenfish as their jaws and small teeth can damage light traces.

Rigs and Tactics:

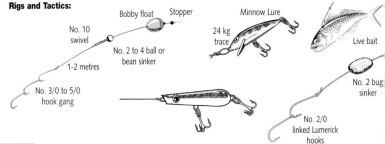

RAINBOW FISH

Scientific name: Family Melanotaeniidae.
Family includes: Blue-eyes, sunfish, rainbow fish.

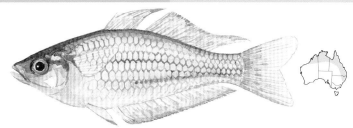

Description: Some of Australia's most colourful native aquarium species are included in the rainbow fish group, including the attractive honey blue-eye (Pseudomugil mellis) and the bright rainbow fishes. The group is recognised by a pointed and flattened snout, large scales, two closely set dorsal fins, the second of which is long and extends to the wrist of the tail and no scales between the pelvic base and the anus on the belly. The anal fin is also long and there is a membrane which joins the pelvic fin to the body of the fish. This group of fishes become more brightly coloured at spawning time, with males much more colourful than females.

REDFIN

Scientific name: Perca fluviatilis.
Also known as English perch, European perch, redfin perch, reddie.

Description: The redfin has prominent scales and five to six prominent vertical stripes which may extend nearly to the belly. These stripes are less prominent in larger fish. The dorsal fin is set well forward and when erect, resembles a small 'sail'. The ventral and anal fins are often very bright red or orange, often with a tinge of white at the ends. The tail fin can also be bright orange, or orange-yellow.

Redfin are often found schooling around drowned timber, at drop-offs near points, or on submerged islands. Redfin prefer cooler water and in summer, the largest fish are almost always below the thermocline in dams or large river holes. Redfin are aggressive and prolific breeders. In impoundments they can stunt out, producing thousands of mature fish as small as 15 cm. In other areas, they can reach 3 kg and provide excellent sport with a variety of techniques.

Fishing: In dams, anchor among drowned timber and bob with bait or lures. A small ball sinker runs to the top of the hook which is baited with worm, cricket, grub or shrimp. The bait is lowered to the bottom and vertically jigged between 30 cm and a metre or so before being dropped to the bottom. Lure casting near drowned timber in large holes in rivers or near drop-offs in rivers or dams is very succesful. Bladed, Celta type lures, diving lures, jigs and small Rapala minnows taking many fish. In WA southern fresh water redfin are the common target species and are a top class sport and feed fish.

Rigs and Tactics:

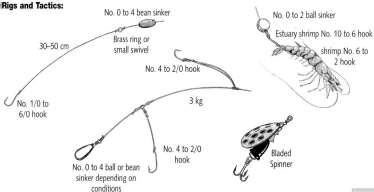

No. 0 to 4 bean sinker

30–50 cm

Brass ring or
small swivel

No. 4 to 2/0 hook

No. 1/0 to
6/0 hook

3 kg

No. 4 to 2/0
hook

No. 0 to 4 ball or bean
sinker depending on
conditions

No. 0 to 2 ball sinker

Estuary shrimp No. 10 to 6 hook

shrimp No. 6 to
2 hook

Bladed
Spinner

RAY, EAGLE

Scientific name: Aetobatus narinari. Also known as Spotted eagle ray, duckbill ray, flying ray, white-spotted eagle ray.

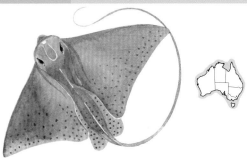

Description: The eagle ray has a shining brown-black top of the body with a large number of white spots on the back half of the body. The eagle ray has an unusual bulging head with a long and tapering snout which is flattened rather like a duck's bill. The teeth are shaped like a chevron and are used for crushing oysters, pipis and other molluscs. The tail is very long and thin and is around 4 times the width of the body. The eagle ray has 2 – 6 barbed spines at the base of the tail. The eagle ray is a very large species, reaching a width of around 3.5 m, but it is commonly seen at around 1.8 metres.

RAY, FIDDLER

Scientific name: Trygonorhina fasciata. Also known as magpie ray, southern fiddler ray.

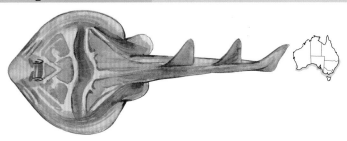

Description: A beautifully marked species, the fiddler ray is actually rarely taken by line fishermen but is often seen in shallow sandy bays throughout its range and can be part of the by-catch of prawn trawlers. The fiddler ray has a brown body covered in a pattern of blue bars often edged in black. The fiddler ray grows to 1.2 m and has a round head region, small flaps and a long tail region. The head shape differs from the shovelnose rays which have a triangular head shape.

RAY, SHOVELNOSE

Scientific name: Rhynchobatus djiddensis. Also known as White-spotted shovelnose ray, fiddler, shovelnose shark, white-spotted guitarfish.

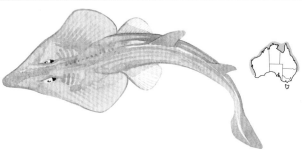

Description: This species is the largest of the shovelnosed rays, generally found in tropical waters and reaching a length of 3 metres. Large adults are dark brown to black whereas smaller individuals are pale brown with white spots on the small flaps and body as far back as the first dorsal fin. Differs from the eastern shovelnose ray (Aptychotrema rostrata) and western shovelnose ray (Aptychotrema vincentiana) which are smaller species reaching 1.2 m and 90 cm respectively in that these species have more rounded body flaps and the first dorsal fin is behind the ventral fins. Fiddler rays have a very round body flap with a protruding shark-like tail. None of these species have spines, or sharp teeth, and are not dangerous.

RIVER BLACKFISH

Scientific name: Gadopsis marmoratus.
Also known as Blackfish, marble cod, slippery, slimy.

Description: The river blackfish is a small elongated native freshwater fish species which is easily identified by the pelvic fins which are reduced to two rays, each of which is divided and finger-like near the end. The dorsal fin is very long and the tail fin is obviously rounded. The mouth is fairly large and the lower jaw is shorter than the upper jaw. This species has a distinctive marbled colouring and fish may vary in colour from almost black, to olive or light brown and there may be obvious purple overtones. The scales are small and the body feels very slimy, giving rise to several alternate common names. River blackfish do not appear to cohabit well with trout and prefer very snaggy waters. They are mainly nocturnal, laying up during the day in cover like hollow logs, which they also use to lay their eggs. The river blackfish can reach over 35 cm, although the two-spined species (which has obvious golden overtones) can reach nearly 5 kg in remote areas.

SAILFISH, INDO-PACIFIC

Scientific name: Istiophorus platypterus. Also known as Pacific sailfish, bayonet fish, sailfish.

Description: The Indo-Pacific sailfish is most easily recognised by the prominent sail-like dorsal fin which when lowered, fits into a groove. The shorter median dorsal rays are still longer than the body is deep. The characteristic upper jaw spear is slender and more than twice the length of the lower jaw.

The ventral rays are very long and extend almost to the anus. The body and sail are spotted with dark and light blue. Indo-Pacific sailfish can reach 120 kg, but any fish over 45 kg is a proud capture.

Fishing: The Indo-Pacific sailfish is a spectacular fish renowned for its spectacular leaps and strong surface runs. The sailfish is one of the smaller billfish but is highly prized, especially as a light line target. Sailfish can be taken by trolling live or dead baits of mullet, mackerel, garfish, rainbow runner or other common medium sized bait fish. Baits enhanced with plastic or feather skirts seem to take more fish. Many fish are taken on lures, including pusher or doorknob type lures or even minnow lures. Sailfish are becoming increasingly targeted with fly gear. Sailfish can travel in small pods and multiple hookups are possible, challenging the skills of all involved. The best sailfishing grounds are undoubtedly off Exmouth, Karratha and Broome in Western Australia, where even fairly small boats can encounter sailfish during peak periods.

Rigs and Tactics:

SALMON, ATLANTIC

Scientific name: Salmo salar.
Also known as Salmon.

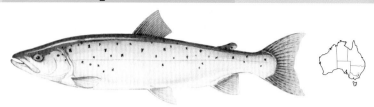

Description: The Atlantic salmon is a generally silvery fish that can have relatively few spots on its body and is often confused even by experienced anglers with silvery, lake coloured brown trout. The most obvious difference (other than location) is that the Atlantic salmon has a tail that while not clearly forked, is obviously indented. The brown trout is frequently called square tail and has a straight tail profile. The caudal peduncle (wrist of tail) is longer than for the similar brown trout.

Atlantic salmon need very cold clean water which is basically unavailable in Australia. In Europe and North America they are the prince of fish but here they are quite slender, with a tendency towards being decidedly skinny and undernourished in NSW, while some smelt feeders in Tasmania can be more robust. In NSW fish over a kilogram, other than released broodfish are rare.

Fishing: Heralded on its introduction as the saviour of freshwater fishing, the Atlantic salmon has been a disastrous experiment for recreational anglers, although it has created a sizeable aquaculture industry in Tasmania. It is only a matter of time before NSW Fisheries stops stocking this species which provides its best fishing in Lake Jindabyne for a few days after older broodstock are released.

Atlantic salmon are taken on standard trout lures and flies while fishing for other species. They prefer fish as food and smelt or gudgeon patterns work best.

Atlantic salmon from Burrinjuck Dam taste very ordinary.

Rigs and Tactics:

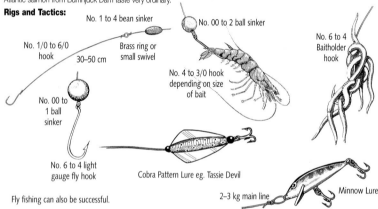

No. 1 to 4 bean sinker

No. 00 to 2 ball sinker

No. 1/0 to 6/0 hook

Brass ring or small swivel

30–50 cm

No. 6 to 4 Baitholder hook

No. 4 to 3/0 hook depending on size of bait

No. 00 to 1 ball sinker

No. 6 to 4 light gauge fly hook

Cobra Pattern Lure eg. Tassie Devil

2–3 kg main line

Minnow Lure

Fly fishing can also be successful.

SOLE, BLACK

Scientific name: Synaptura nigra.

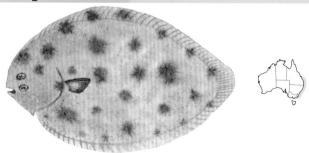

Description: All the true soles in Australia are right-eyed. Their eyes migrate to the right side of their bodies as they develop when small juveniles. The similar lemon-tongue sole (Paraplagusia unicolor) is a lefteyed fish and has a diagnostic hook to the snout. The black sole is very round shaped and does not have a defined tail. The black sole prefers sandy or sandy-mud bottoms of coastal shallows and large estuaries and grows to a length of 35 centimetres.

SALMON, AUSTRALIAN

Scientific name: Arripis truttucca.

Also known as Salmon, black back, cocky salmon, colonial salmon, kahawai. Salmon trout and bay trout, (juveniles).

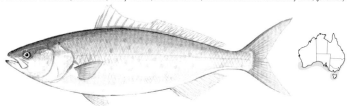

Description: The 'salmon' is not related to true trout and salmon in the family Salmonidae and are more closely related to the mullets. Australian salmon reaches 9 kg. The forked tail of adult salmon is dark, and the eye is generally yellow. The body is classically torpedo shaped and full of power. The head, and the mouth are moderately large. There are distinctive brown spots or dashes along the dorsal surface although the larger specimens become dark across the back. The belly is silvery to white. The Australian salmon moves along the south coast in summer and up the west coast reaching Perth in small numbers around Easter.

Fishing: The Australian salmon is one of the best light tackle sportsfish in Australia. They are the best fighting fish taken from the beach, where their strong runs and spectacular leaps more than compensate for the average eating quality. Australian salmon form large schools making them vulnerable to commercial fishing. There is little doubt that commercial fishing can affect local abundance and recreational fishing quality. These schools can provide spectacular fishing, but on occasions these schooling fish will not feed. Australian salmon are frequently caught on pilchards and cut baits, with belly fillets or baits with white skin attached doing better. Pipis, cockles and beach worms work and can surprise whiting fisherman. In estuaries, salmon trout are often taken on whitebait, blue bait, prawns or squid. The bite of the salmon is frequently quite fumbling and some patience is required before setting the hook.

Rigs and Tactics:

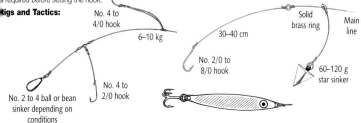

SALMON, COOKTOWN

Scientific name: Eleutheronema tetradactylum. Also known as Threadfin, giant threadfin, blue salmon, Rockhampton kingfish.

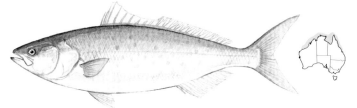

Description: Even reliable reference books provide confusing information on the status of the various threadfin salmon species. The Cooktown salmon is the largest of these distinctive species which are easily identified by the unusual overshot upper jaw and absence of lips around a large mouth. The threadfin salmon species have an unusual body shape as the body is thickest through the second dorsal fin. The most obvious diagnostic feature is the divided pectoral fin with its separate, finger-like filaments. The Cooktown salmon has four separate, and shorter pectoral filaments as opposed to five in the threadfin salmon (see below). These fish are commonly found in estuaries, where they can range up to the tidal limit in creeks and rivers. They are also found close to shore, near jetties, in harbours or over coastal tidal mud or sand flats. The Cooktown salmon can reach 1.2 m and up to 18 kilograms.

Rigs and Tactics:

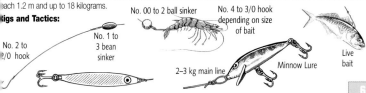

SALMON, THREADFIN

Scientific name: Polydactylus sheridani
Also known as Blue threadfin, blue salmon
Burnett salmon, king salmon.

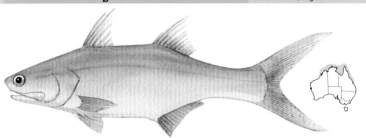

Description: The threadfin salmon is similar to the Cooktown salmon, but possesses 5 long, distinctive fingers on the lower edge of the pectoral fin. This species has a more pronounced blue colour and a long and relatively narrow caudal wrist. The threadfin salmon is common between 0.5 and around 3 kg with occasional specimens slightly larger.
Another similar species, the Northern or striped threadfin salmon (Polydactylus plebius) is separated by its more prominent stripes and overall golden colour and five free filaments, of which the two uppermost are longest.

Rigs and Tactics:

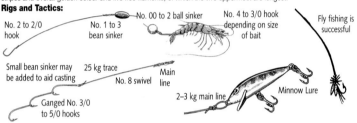

No. 2 to 2/0 hook

No. 1 to 3 bean sinker

No. 00 to 2 ball sinker

No. 4 to 3/0 hook depending on size of bait

Fly fishing is successful

Small bean sinker may be added to aid casting

25 kg trace

No. 8 swivel

Main line

Ganged No. 3/0 to 5/0 hooks

2–3 kg main line

Minnow Lure

SWEEP, SEA

Scientific name: Scorpis aequipinnis. Also known as Sweep.

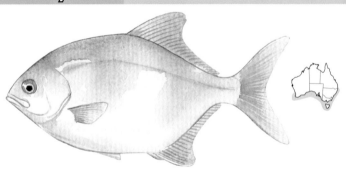

Description: The sea sweep is a deep bodied fish quite common on deeper reefs of the south coast and south-west of Australia, but which can also be found inshore, especially in schools when young. The sea sweep is generally slate grey in colour. It may have two darker grey patches on the upper body above the back edge of the pectoral fin and also the back part of the dorsal fin. This species has a prominent lobe to the first dorsal ray whereas the similar silver sweep (Scorpis lineolatus) has a flat dorsal fin profile. The mouth extends to the middle of the eye in the sea sweep and only to the front edge of the eye in the silver sweep. The banded sweep (Scorpis georgianus) has prominent black bands, a lightly forked tail and is only found from Kangaroo Island in South Australia to Shark Bay in Western Australia. The sea sweep can reach 61 cm and more than 3.5 kilograms.

Fishing: In its smaller sizes, the sweep is frequently considered a pest. Its small mouth, schooling nature and fondness for picking baits intended for larger species has earned the sea sweep a poor reputation in some areas. However, in larger sizes sea sweep make good eating and are a welcome addition to mixed bags. As a rule, the larger fish are found in smaller groups and further offshore, with bait picking juveniles inshore. Sea sweep will take a variety of baits, with prawns, squid, cuttlefish and fresh cut fish baits working best. Smaller, long shank hooks will improve your hookup rate. If pickers are prominent, putting a smaller hook on a dropper above your standard snapper rigs will tell you the nature of the bait stealers. Small sea sweep make a hardy live bait for fish like kingfish or samsonfish.

SAMSON FISH

Scientific name: Seriola hippos.
Also known as Sambo, samson, sea kingfish.

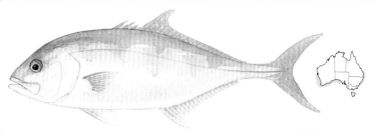

Description: A large and powerful fish capable of reaching 1.8 m and more than 50 kg in weight. Similar in appearance to the closely related yellowtail kingfish, but the samson fish is a much cleaner fighter which does not usually bury the angler on any available reef. The samson fish is best separated by counting the second dorsal rays which has 23–25 as opposed to 31 or over for yellowtail kingfish. The 16–17 anal rays on the samson fish distinguish this species from the amberjack which has 19 or more anal rays and 29 to 35 second dorsal rays. The samson fish also has a more rounded forehead which is more pronounced in younger fish.

The flesh surrounding the teeth in both jaws in the samson fish is often but not always engorged with blood, giving the tooth patches a red appearance. The colour varies but the samson fish can often have distinct vertical blotches which, while fading with age, are not found in the other similar species.

Fishing: A real challenge on light gear as skillful handling can present some extremely large fish due to their relatively clean, strong fight. Samson fish can be taken at all depths from nearshore waters to around 30 fathoms. They can be found near and patches, around reefs or seagrass and can take whiting, garfish or other small fish from surprised anglers. Best baits are live fish, whole fresh dead fish, fillets, pilchard, octopus, squid or crabs. Samson fish can be taken on deep vertical fished jigs and rarely on trolled lures. Small samson fish make good eating, but large fish over 15 kg are best returned to fight another day. Large fish in particular can be infected with a parasite which causes the flesh to virtually disintegrate on cooking.

Rigs and Tactics:

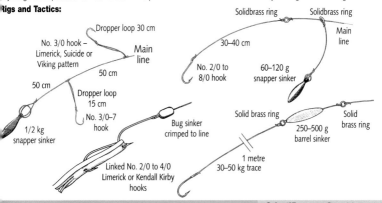

SPOTTED WOBBEGONG

Scientific name: Orectolobus maculatus. Also known as Common catshark, tassel shark.

Description: The spotted wobbegong shark inhabits coastal and estuarine reefs of cooler waters, being most common in NSW. Wobbegongs are easily identified by the numerous fleshy tentacle-like appendages around the front of the rounded head. This species is identified by two wart-like protrusions above each eye and the large pale-edged spots which resemble eyes on the dorsal surface. The spotted wobbegong can reach 3.2 m and is harmless except when disturbed by divers. There have been some instances where large wobbegongs have felt trapped in small caves by divers and attacked. There was an attack at Shellharbour in NSW, where a silver face mask attracted a bite requiring numerous stitches.

SARATOGA, SOUTHERN

Scientific name: Scleropages leichardti. Also known as spotted barramundi spotted saratoga, Dawson river salmon.

Description: The southern saratoga is similar to the gulf saratoga, but the mouth is slightly smaller and the large scales carry two or more red spots which form a vertical streak. The protruding lower jaw carries two small barbels near the lower lip. The pectoral fins are large and extend to the start of the small pelvic fins. The southern saratoga is much lighter through the body than the gulf saratoga and consequently weighs much less for the same length.

The saratogas belong to a family commonly known as the bony tongue fishes, which means that the bony mouth can be difficult to set a hook into.

The southern saratoga naturally inhabits fairly turbid streams, but they adapt well to impoundments and provide additional sport for keen lure and fly fishers.

Fishing: The southern saratoga is becoming an increasingly prized species for specimen fly anglers who value the challenge of spotting and landing this fish. They will rise readily to large surface flies such as the Dahlberg diver and fight hard and spectacularly. Saratoga will also take lures very well, especially surface lures or shallow running lures. Live frogs and unweighted shrimps cast near cruising fish are successful.

The saratoga is very poor eating and is much more highly regarded as a sport fish. The very small number of eggs (only 70 to 200) produced by a female means that each fish is valuable and should be carefully looked after.

Rigs and Tactics:

Fly fishing is successful

Minnow Lure

Freshwater popper

No. 00 to 2 ball sinker

No. 4 to 3/0 hook depending on size of bait

SNOOK

Scientific name: Sphyraena novaehollandiae.
Also known as Short finned sea pike, sea pike, short finned barracuda.

Description: It is easily separated from the barracuda by its southern range and the first dorsal fin which commences well behind the end of the pectoral fin. The snook is similar to the long finned sea pike but most easily separated by the snook's shorter anal fin, and its ventral fins which are set well behind the pectoral fin. The snook reaches 1.1 m and 5 kilograms and is a highly regarded sportfish. It is often trolled with chrome lures over inshore weed beds.

Fishing: The snook is relatively common in inshore cooler waters with a distinct preference for areas of weed or sand areas adjacent to weed or slight drop offs. The snook is an ambush feeder which may hunt in small packs, providing exciting fishing at times. Snook also favour regular haunts and may be found in identified hot-spots on a regular basis. Snook will take baits of whitebait, pilchard, bluebait, cut flesh or squid. Over shallow weed beds, lightly weighted or unweighted baits on single hooks or gang hook rigs work best and a gentle jigging action attracts additional strikes. Over deeper waters, or where snook may be holed up a small running sinker with a short trace to defend against the teeth will work well. Snook take lures and flies well. Best bets are silver or chrome spoons such as Tobys, or Wonder Wobblers. Feather jigs and small minnow lures also work well but the toothy mouth of the snook means that some fish can be lost to short strikes and lures and flies damaged. The snook makes good to excellent eating although the flesh is little soft and may bruise unless handled well.

SERGEANT BAKER

Scientific name: Aulopus purpurissatus.

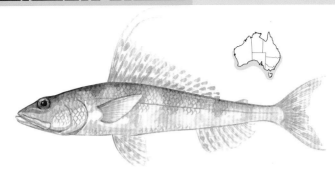

Description: A reasonably common fish of deeper coastal reefs and adjacent sandy patches, but can move into larger bays on occasion. Sergeant baker have a red, ruddy or rusty brown colour and a small adipose-like second dorsal fin. The longer first dorsal fin unusually does not have any spines, only soft rays and the second and third ray is elongated in male fish.

The caudal fin is forked and the pectoral fins are large but the sergeant baker lacks the distinctive 'fingers' or bony head ridges of the gurnards. The sergeant baker reaches 70 cm in length and around 3 kg, but is more common at around 45 to 50 centimetres.

Fishing: Sergeant baker are taken on standard bottom bouncing rigs adjacent to mid to deep water reefs. Sergeant baker prefer fresh fish fillets, pilchards, squid, octopus, prawn, or crab baits, but the large mouth does not prevent them from being taken on quite large live or dead baits. Sergeant baker can also be taken on bait tipped jigs.

The flesh is white but only fair compared to other species like snapper or morwong taken from the same areas and can have a muddy taste.

Rigs and Tactics:

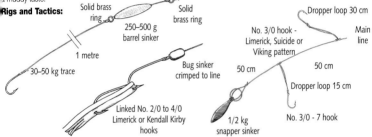

Solid brass ring

250–500 g barrel sinker

Solid brass ring

1 metre

30–50 kg trace

Bug sinker crimped to line

Linked No. 2/0 to 4/0 Limerick or Kendall Kirby hooks

Dropper loop 30 cm

No. 3/0 hook - Limerick, Suicide or Viking pattern

50 cm

Main line

50 cm

Dropper loop 15 cm

1/2 kg snapper sinker

No. 3/0 - 7 hook

SHARK, PORT JACKSON

Scientific name: Heterodontus portusjacksoni. Also known as Bull shark, horn shark.

Description: The Port Jackson shark is a harmless species of inshore reefs and adjacent sand and weed patches which may group together in large numbers. The Port Jackson shark is an extremely primitive species readily identifiable by the bony ridge above the eye and a strong dorsal spine in front of both dorsal fins. The teeth are small and pointed in the front of the jaws with crushing teeth to the rear. The Port Jackson shark lays the distinctive 'Mermaid's purse' egg case which is attached to kelp and is frequently washed up on beaches after storms. The Port Jackson shark can reach 2 m but is more common at around a metre.

SHARK, BLACK-TIPPED REEF

Scientific name: Carcharhinus melanopterus.

Also known as blacktip, reef shark.

Description: A small but easily identified whaler species reaching around 1.8 metres. The black-tipped reef shark has an obvious black tip to all of its fins, including both lobes of the tail. This is the only species with a black tip to the dorsal fin. The black-tipped reef shark is found on reef country and is an active hunter. They will move up onto very shallow on a rising tide searching for food with their dorsal fins and even their backs scything through the water. They often travel in groups and can be quite disconcerting for swimmers or divers. They are considered to be one of the least dangerous of the whaler species, but caution should always be exercised, especially in groups of fish or where blood is in the water.

SHARK, BRONZE WHALER

Scientific name: Carcharhinus brachyurus. Also known as Copper shark, cocktail shark.

Description: A fairly common shark of offshore waters, but which occasionally enters large embayments. The bronze whaler is dangerous and has been responsible for several fatalities in Australia. The bronze whaler is very similar to the black or whaler shark but the bronze whaler generally has a bronze or coppery colour, which fades to grey after death. The upper teeth are narrow and slightly concave on this species. The bronze whaler lacks the distinctive skin ridge running between the two dorsal fins which is present on the black whaler. The bronze whaler reaches 3.25 m and more than 200 kilograms.

SHARK, GREY NURSE

Scientific name: Carcharias taurus. Also known as Grey nurse.

Description: Easily recognised by the two similar sized dorsal fins and the rows of long fang-like teeth which have two small cusps near the base. This species is familiar to many as it is often kept in larger aquariums where its impressive teeth and relatively placid nature make it an ideal attraction for viewers and divers.

Black Rock in NSW is well known for its grey nurse sharks. The grey nurse shark can exceed 3.5 m, but they look considerably larger in aquariums. The species is subject to much emotive controversy in NSW.

SHARK, GUMMY

Scientific name: Mustelus antarcticus.
Also known as Sweet William.

Description: The gummy shark is a small, harmless shark reaching only 1.75 metres. The teeth in both jaws are smooth and flattened and arranged in a flat pavement-like pattern. The gummy shark looks similar to the school shark, but the school shark's teeth are sharp and triangular and the tail fin has a broad and deeply notched upper lobe, giving a double tail appearance. The upper body of the gummy shark is covered with small white spots which are less apparent in larger fish.

Fishing: The gummy shark is frequently taken by anglers on deeper water snapper grounds with standard snapper baits and rigs. The gummy shark is more common on deeper water grounds and is a commercial fishing target which has been seriously overfished in many southern waters. The gummy shark can move into shallow water on occasion. The best baits for gummy shark are squid, cuttlefish, octopus, pilchard and any fresh fish baits. They are most often taken on the bottom hook of a snapper paternoster rig. The gummy shark makes excellent eating and is highly regarded.

Rigs and Tactics:

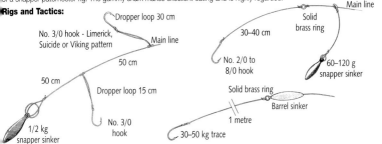

SHARK, WHITE POINTER

Scientific name: Carcharodon carcharias. Also known as Great white shark, white shark, white death.

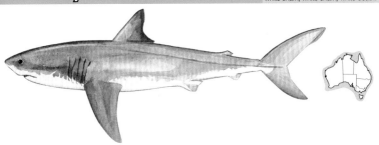

Description: The white pointer shark is a large and extremely dangerous species and the star of the Jaws movies which has lead to the misguided destruction of many harmless sharks. However, the white pointer is responsible for more attacks on humans than any other species. The white pointer, reaches 6.4 m and more than 1200 kilograms. As in most shark species, males are smaller and easily identified by the claspers which assist in copulation.

The white pointer shark has a conical snout, long gill slits and extremely sharp, serrated triangular teeth. The colour is generally grey to dark grey above with a white belly.

The white pointer prefers oceanic waters and does not often move close inshore, except to breed or to follow seal colonies when pups are produced. They are more commonly found inshore along the south coast but have been observed off Perth beaches in recent years. There is much more danger involved in driving to the beach than from a shark while swimming, but the white death evokes a primitive fear in many, many people.

Fishing: The white pointer is now totally protected. There are special procedures for the few fish which are hooked by recreational fishers.

White pointers were viewed as the ultimate capture for game fishermen, with many young recreational fishers being aware of Bob Dyer's 1062 kg fish from Moreton Island and Alf Dean's 1208 kg fish in 1960 from South Australia.

SHARK, MAKO

Scientific name: Isurus oxyrinchus.
Also known as Shortfin mako, blue pointer, jumping shark.

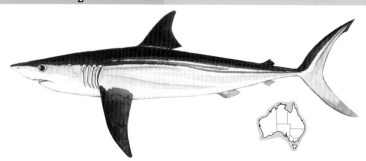

Description: The mako shark is a sleek, beautifully streamlined close relative of the great white. The mako differs from the great white in being more streamlined and having distinctly pointed and hooked upper teeth as opposed to the distinctly triangular teeth in the great white. The mako is distinctly blue in colour though this fades to grey-blue after death. The pectoral fin is shorter than in the blue shark. The mako prefers deep offshore waters, but can move into more coastal waters where its sleek form and hooked teeth make short work of any hooked fish. If the hooked fish is skull dragged past the mako, it can provoke an attack on the boat, leaving teeth in the hull and very shaken fishermen. The mako is the most prized shark for game fishing, but is extremely dangerous for small boat fishermen.

Fishing: The mako shark is the most prized shark species for game fishermen. The strong fight and leaps of up to 6 m add to the excitement of taking them. Very good quality tackle is required and live or fresh dead fish baits will increase chances of a hook-up. The mako responds well to berley, especially near deep water current lines or schools of mackerel. The mako is extremely dangerous for small boat fishermen as they can attack boats, jump into boats while still 'green', causing incredible damage, or even while seemingly dead they can muster energy to trash a small cockpit with slashing teeth and tail.

The mako is reasonable eating in small to medium sizes but should be bled and put on ice to prevent a build-up of ammonia in the flesh.

Rigs and Tactics:

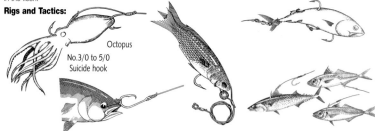

Octopus
No.3/0 to 5/0
Suicide hook

SHARK, HAMMERHEAD

Scientific name: Sphyrna lewini.
Also known as Scalloped
hammerhead shark.

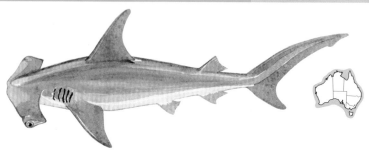

Description: There is absolutely no mistaking the hammerhead shark, whose distinctive, broad head is unique. The scalloped hammerhead shark can reach 6 m but is more common at around 3 metres. This species has a distinctive groove at the front edge of the hammer, which extends to the nostrils, which are near the eyes. They are common offshore, but can enter bays and inlets. The smooth headed hammerhead lacks the distinctive groove or notch and reaches around 4 m in the colder water it prefers.

SHARK, TIGER

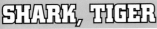

Scientific name: Galeocerdo cuvier.

Description: A large and extremely dangerous species of shark. The tiger shark can be found well offshore and can venture into the surf zone on occasions, especially during breeding season. The characteristic colour pattern of the tiger shark is a tiger-like series of bars on the upper body. The teeth are unusually shaped, being large and pointed backwards, with strong serrations, especially on the back edge. Although the colouring and shape are distinctive, a dive charter at Ningaloo Reef, with a boat load of tourists, attempted to dive with a tiger shark they thought was a whale shark. The shark, like many when well fed and not threatened, was docile and there was no real incident. The tiger shark can reach nearly 6.5 m and more than 00 kilograms.

Fishing: The tiger shark is a famous visitor to the old whaling stations of Australia, where large numbers of tigers, would attack whale carcasses waiting to be flensed. Tiger sharks are attracted by berley and are taken with very large dead baits, especially those with oily or bloody flesh. The tiger shark is a powerful and dogged opponent and is sought by some specialist gamefishermen. Taking any large shark from small boats requires enormous preparation and should not be attempted by any inexperienced angler. The tiger shark is a large and opportunistic feeder which will attack humans and should be treated with extreme caution. If sharks are not being targeted and a large tiger shark shows up – move.

Rigs and Tactics:

SHARK, SCHOOL

Scientific name: Galeorhinus galeus. Also known as Snapper shark, eastern school shark, greyboy, grey shark, soupfin shark, tope.

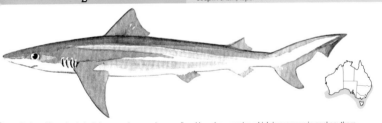

Description: The school shark is a very slow growing, small and harmless species which is common in cool southern waters. It is more common in offshore areas, where it forms the basis of a substantial, but overfished commercial fishery. Juveniles may occasionally be found in coastal bays. This species is readily identified by the tail fin shape, which has the upper lobe broad and deeply notched, giving the appearance of a double tail. The dorsal fin is set well forward and is closer to the commencement of the pectoral than the ventral fins. Both jaws carry sharp, triangular teeth of similar size which immediately separates the school shark from the gummy shark with its smooth and flattened teeth. The school shark can reach 2 m and 60 kg but is commonly much smaller. School sharks can live more than 40 years and a tagged fish had grown only 18 cm in over 35 years at liberty.

Rigs and Tactics:

Dropper loop 30 cm
No. 3/0 to 6/0 hook - Suicide or Viking pattern
50 cm
50 cm
Main line
1/2 kg snapper sinker
Dropper loop 15 cm
No. 3/0 - 6/0 hook

Main line
Solid brass ring
30–40 cm
No. 2/0 to 6/0 hook
60–120 g snapper sinker

SKATE, MELBOURNE

Scientific name: Raja whitleyi.
Also known as Whitley's skate, great skate.

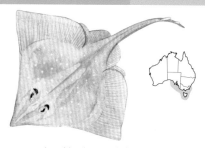

Description: All skates lack the venomous spines of the stingrays and stingarees.

This species is the largest, reaching 50 kg and 1.7 metres. The Melbourne skate is common in shallow coastal waters but is most commonly caught in trawls. The upper surface is brownish-grey and flecked with white. The undersurface of the triangular snout is a similar colour. In the smaller thornback skate (Raja lemprieri) which is common in Tasmania, the underside of the snout is black. The upper surface is covered with sharp denticles with the largest on either side of the midline whereas the thornback skate has a row of prominent spines along the backbone.

Fishing: Baits must be fished on the bottom with standard bottom fishing rigs over sand or other soft bottom. Baits include squid, prawns, cut fish or worm baits. In common with all dorsally compressed species, skates put up an extremely powerful if unspectacular fight. They can sit on the bottom until the frustrated angler breaks the line. Skates are very good eating, with the wings being very tasty and passable 'mock' scallops can be made with a round cookie cutter.

Rigs and Tactics:

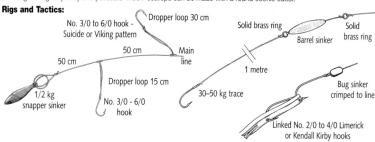

SNAPPER, QUEEN

Scientific name: Nemadactylus valenciennesi.
Also known as southern blue morwong.

Description: A handsome representative of the morwong family, the queen snapper is often a rich blue colour. There are distinctive yellow lines on the face and around the eyes and there is usually a large black blotch in the middle of the side of the fish. The queen snapper has the extended rays of the pectoral fin like many of the morwongs. The tail fin is deeply forked. The queen snapper is found from inshore reefs to a depth of 240 m and has a preference for reef country.

Fishing: The queen snapper is a beautiful and much prized catch for reef fishermen in cooler waters. They are taken from similar areas and with the same rigs as for pink snapper, although queen snapper are more often taken from the shallower reefs than pinkies. The queen snapper has a smaller mouth with the typical morwong lips and therefore slightly smaller hooks are recommended if queen snapper are the target species. Queen snapper are taken on squid, octopus, cut baits, pilchards, prawn or crab baits. The queen snapper is considered to be very good eating, especially from the cooler waters of the south coast. The queen snapper can reach one metre in length.

SNAPPER

Scientific name: Pagrus auratus. (formerly Chrysophrys auratus) Also known as schnapper, Pink snapper and pinkie. With increasing size known as Cockney bream, red bream, squire, snapper and ultimately 'old man snapper' with the characteristic hump.

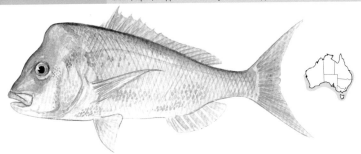

Description: A truly stunning and highly sought after species, the snapper can have iridescent pink to burnished copper colouration with bright blue spots from the lateral line upwards which are brightest in younger fish. A hump on the head and nose area develops in some fish and is more likely in male fish. Snapper are relatively slow growing and mature at 29 to 35 cm and four to five years of age. Snapper numbers have been affected by both commercial and recreational overfishing.

Fishing: Snapper are traditionally taken on bottom paternoster rigs with the famous snapper lead. Snapper prefer the edges of reefs or broken ground and can be taken from the shore or as deep as 50 fathoms. Drifting over broken ground or drop-offs at the edges of reefs with just enough weight to bounce bottom will find fish and repeated drifts will pick up more fish. Like many reef species, snapper form s of similar sized fish, with the size of the school decreasing with larger fish.

In late winter on the east coast, snapper move inshore to feed on spawning cuttlefish and large fish can be taken from the rocks on cuttlefish baits.

Quality snapper can be taken by sinking a bait under a feeding school of tailor, salmon or small mackerel. Snapper are a magnificent fighting fish and are excellent eating, but do not freeze particularly well.

Rigs and Tactics:

Dropper loop 30 cm

No. 3/0 to 6/0 hook -
Suicide or Viking pattern

Main line

50 cm

50 cm

Dropper loop 15 cm

No. 3/0
to 6/0 hook

1/2 kg
snapper sinker

Solid
brass ring

Main line

30–40 cm

No. 2/0 to
8/0 hook

60–120 g
snapper sinker

Bug sinker
crimped to
line

No.3/0 to 5/0
Suicide hook

Small octopus

Linked No. 2/0 to 4/0 Limerick or
Kendall Kirby hooks

SNAPPER, RED

Scientific name: Centroberyx gerrardi.
Also known as Bight redfish.

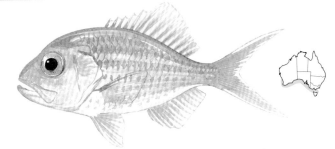

Description: The red snapper is most commonly a species of deeper reefs in cooler southern waters which may range from shallow reefs to more than 300 metres. A handsome species very similar to the smaller nannygai but is able to be separated by having 6 dorsal fin spines versus 7 in the nannygai. The red snapper has a distinctive white line along the lateral line and white margins on the fins. The head is also less rounded than in the nannygai. The eye is generally red but can fade to red-silver after death. The red snapper can reach 66 cm, but is more common at 40 – 45 centimetres. It is found singly in larger sizes or in small groups when smaller.

TAILOR

Scientific name: Pomatomus saltatrix.
Also known as Tailer, chopper, bluefish (USA), elf (South Africa), skipjack.

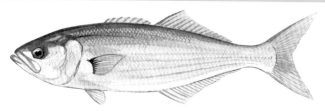

Description: The tailor is a renowned predatory species best known for its relatively small but extremely sharp teeth. The tailor has a moderately forked tail, and a bluish to blue-green back which changes to more silvery and white on the belly. The eye can be yellow. The fins vary in colour but the tail fin is usually darker than the others.

Juvenile tailor are found in estuaries and embayments. Larger tailor move to the beaches and inshore reefs at between 25 – 35 centimetres. Tailor undergo a spawning migration, finishing at Fraser Island in Queensland. Tailor can reach 10 kg with any fish over 5 kg being rightly claimed as a prize and fish over 1.5 kg being large. Tailor are voracious feeders, with individual fish gorging themselves before regurgitating to continue in a feeding frenzy.

Fishing: Tailor are a highly prized species which readily takes a bait, fights hard and, if bled immediately after capture make fine eating. Tailor can be taken from boat or shore, on lure, fly or bait and by anglers of any skill level.

The most common bait and rig would be a whole pilchard bait on a gang hook rig. In the surf and where casting distance is required, a sliding sinker rig works best, with a star or spoon sinker on a dropper trace doing well. In estuaries, from a boat, or in calmer surf, an unweighted or minimally weighted bait provides by far the best results. Tailor readily feed high in the water column and avidly attack a floating bait. Another rig which works well is to use a nearly filled plastic bubble to gain casting distance without rapidly sinking the bait. Tailor bite best at dusk and dawn.

Tailor smoke very well and are fair eating when fresh. The flesh of the tailor is fairly oily and bruises easily. Tailor makes a quality cut bait.

Rigs and Tactics:

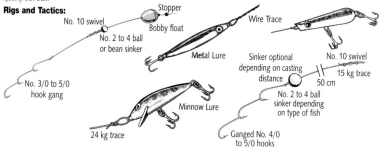

TARPON

Scientific name: Megalops cyprinoides. Also known as Oxeye herring.

Description: The tarpon is most easily identified by the long trailing filament at the rear of the single dorsal fin. The eye is also very large as are the upper jaw bones. The tail is deeply forked and powerful. The scales are very large. Tarpon are commonly found in mangrove creeks, larger estuaries and bays. The tarpon can grow to 1.5 m and around 3.5 kilograms.

Fishing: The tarpon will take dead fish bait but can be very finicky. They can sometimes be taken on small live baits. However, tarpon are a fantastic fighting fish and are a target species for lure and fly fishers. Most fish are taken on small white jigs or small chrome lures. They are also avid fly takers. The mouth of the tarpon is bony and hooks should be at their absolute sharpest to get a solid hookup that can survive the strong fight and aerial display of the tarpon. Tarpon are extremely bony and are considered poor eating. Care should be taken with handling to reduce scale loss and long term mortality of released fish.

TARWHINE

Scientific name: Rhabdosargus sarba.
Also known as Silver bream.

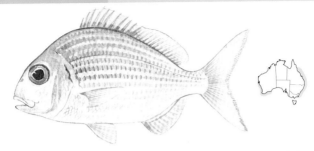

Description: The tarwhine is similar to the various bream species but differs in a few key areas. The tarwhine has a number of thin golden or brown stripes running the length of the otherwise silver body. The nose of the tarwhine is blunt and there are 11 or 12 anal rays whereas bream have 9 or fewer. The fins other than the dorsal fin are generally bright yellow or yellow-orange and the tarwhine has a black lining to its gut cavity. Tarwhine are common in inshore and estuarine areas and may be found on offshore reefs on occasions. Tarwhine form schools, especially in smaller sizes. They can reach 80 cm and more than 3 kg but they are most commonly caught at a few hundred grams.

Fishing: Tarwhine can be voracious feeders, taking a wide variety of baits including cut flesh, bluebait, whitebait and parts of pilchard but many more are caught on prawn, pipi, worm, nipper or squid baits. Tarwhine are also occasionally taken on cabbage baits by luderick and drummer fishermen in NSW.

While tarwhine bite very hard, their relatively small mouth and frequent small size makes them nuisance bait pickers in many instances. Use a smaller hook for better results, but don't let the fish run with the bait too far as they can easily become gut hooked. In estuaries or shallow waters, a light running ball sinker rig works best while off the rocks or in deeper water, use as little weight and as light a rig as you can get away with. Tarwhine fight well for their size. They also make very good eating although they can have an iodine taste if not bled immediately and the guts and black stomach lining removed as soon as possible.

Rigs and Tactics:

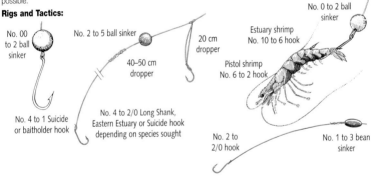

No. 00 to 2 ball sinker

No. 4 to 1 Suicide or baitholder hook

No. 2 to 5 ball sinker

40–50 cm dropper

No. 4 to 2/0 Long Shank, Eastern Estuary or Suicide hook depending on species sought

20 cm dropper

No. 0 to 2 ball sinker

Estuary shrimp
No. 10 to 6 hook

Pistol shrimp
No. 6 to 2 hook

No. 2 to 2/0 hook

No. 1 to 3 bean sinker

TREVALLA, DEEP SEA

Scientific name: Hyperoglyphe antarctica. Also known as Blue-eyed trevalla, blue eye cod, big eye, bluenose, medusa fish.

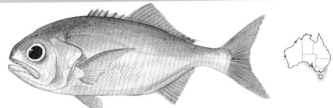

Description: The deep sea trevalla is a deeper water species which is taken in depths of up to 300 fathoms. It undergoes quite a dramatic change in form as it grows. Juveniles are often found associated with large jellyfish and have quite rounded fins which become angular, especially the tail of adults. Deep sea trevalla have a large deep blue eye with a golden ring. The large eye is typical of deeper predatory species. The mouth is large and this species is best separated from the similar but smaller warehou or the spotted trevalla (Seriolella punctata) by the more steeply sloping forehead and lack of spots in the deep sea trevalla. The deep sea trevalla reaches 1.4 metres and nearly 40 kilograms while the warehou grows to 76 cm and around 7 kilograms. The second dorsal of the deep sea trevalla is shorter and has 15 – 21 rays versus 25 or more for the other trevalla species.

TERAGLIN

Scientific name: Atractoscion aequidens.
Also known as Trag, trag-jew.

Description: The teraglin is very similar to the mulloway but can be separated by the shape of the tail, which is slightly concave (inwards curving) in the teraglin and convex (outward curving) in the mulloway. The inside of the teraglin's mouth is yellow or orange and this extends to the inside of the gill covers and occasionally to the lips. The anal fin is closer to the tail fin in the teraglin but this is only obvious when the two are seen together. The teraglin reaches a smaller size than mulloway, growing to up to a metre and 10 kg but any fish over 5 – 6 kg is considered large. The teraglin is found on offshore reefs and commonly forms schools which are smaller in number for larger fish.

Fishing: The teraglin is commonly caught in depths of 20 to 80 m and over broken reef, although they can be found on the edge of larger deep reefs or on gravel bottom.

Unlike mulloway, teraglin are rarely found inshore and not in estuaries. Teraglin most common on the bottom but can be found in mid-water, especially when berley is used. Teraglin feed much more strongly at night and an area that produces nothing during the day can produce large catches of trag after dark. Teraglin bite best on small live baits or large strip baits with squid, cuttlefish, pilchard and large prawns also producing fish.

Teraglin bite strongly and heavy lines are frequently used so that the fish are brought to boat quickly as a lost fish can often take the school with them. The school will often rise with hooked fish, enabling them to be taken in mid water. Common two hook snapper rigs are most commonly used for teraglin.

As teraglin frequently school in the same areas, they are susceptible to over-fishing and only as many as are needed should be taken. Teraglin are excellent eating, with many rating them better quality than mulloway.

Rigs and Tactics:

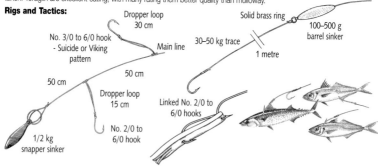

TRIPLE TAIL

Scientific name: Lobotes surinamensis.
Also known as Jumping cod.

Description: The tripletail is a reasonably large predator of mangrove creeks, estuaries and inshore reefs which can reach 1 m and around 11 kg but is more common at smaller sizes. The most obvious feature is the elongated soft dorsal and anal fins which gives the resemblance of three tails. The base colour varies from yellow in small juveniles to chocolate brown with a silvery sheen and there may be grey mottling. The eye is relatively small and the mouth is also fairly small finishing in front of the eye.

TOADFISH, WEEPING

Scientific name: Torquigener pleurogramma. Also known as blowie, common blowfish.

Caution

POISONOUS

Description: This is a fairly small species only reaching 22 cm and commonly found in sandy surf areas and around jetties and pylons where they are many children's first fish. The diagnostic feature is the single dark brown stripe down the side and up to six narrow dark bands which run downwards across the cheek and near the eye, giving the appearance of tear stains. Like all toadfish, the banded toadfish can inflate its abdomen with air or water and small rough spikelets are extended.

Fishing: The weeping toadfish, in common with the other similar toadfish species can be caught on a variety of small baits, which can fit into the small mouth with its sharp fused teeth. This species can occur in plague proportions in many estuaries and are widely despised. They should never be kept and consumed or fed to domestic pets as there have been a number of fatalities, including humans. The toxins are strongest in the skin and internal organs, especially the liver.

Rigs and Tactics: Not applicable as Toadfish are not recommended as an angling species.

TRIGGERFISH, STARRY

Scientific name: Abalistes stellaris.

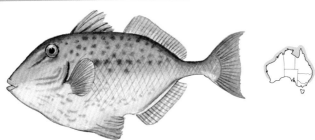

Description: The triggerfish are similar to the leatherjackets but differ in two obvious features. Triggerfish have three obvious dorsal spines in the first dorsal while leatherjackets have two of which the second is only rudimentary. Triggerfish also have obvious scales whereas leatherjackets have rough skin without obvious scales. The starry triggerfish is one of the largest triggerfish species, reaching 60 centimetres. It is the triggerfish most frequently taken by recreational anglers. The mouth is small in the large head. The colour is pale and the common name comes from three white blotches on the back and a scattering of white spots on the upper body. There are yellow spots on the lower body. There are two small trailing filaments on both lobes of the tail in adults.

Fishing: This species is not a target species but is taken by line fishers, mainly in tropical reef areas. The small mouth means that small or long shanked hooks improve catch rates. Best baits are prawns, crab, squid or cut baits. Triggerfish are often regarded as a pest due to their ability to steal baits and avoid hook-ups. Triggerfish are reasonable eating but should be skinned.

Rigs and Tactics:

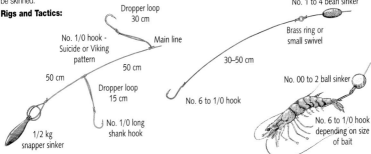

Dropper loop
30 cm

No. 1/0 hook -
Suicide or Viking
pattern

Main line

50 cm

50 cm

Dropper loop
15 cm

No. 1/0 long
shank hook

1/2 kg
snapper sinker

No. 1 to 4 bean sinker

Brass ring or
small swivel

30–50 cm

No. 6 to 1/0 hook

No. 00 to 2 ball sinker

No. 6 to 1/0 hook
depending on size
of bait

TREVALLY, BRASSY

Scientific name: Caranx papuensis.
Also known as Papuan trevally.

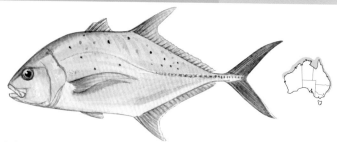

Description: The brassy trevally is a very similar species to the giant trevally and is often misdescribed in fishing publications. The brassy trevally is often in schools of similar sized fish on inshore tidal areas or reef edges where they they often ambush feed. The brassy trevally has a white rear border to the lower lobe of the tail fin and sometimes the rear of the anal fin which separates it from the giant trevally. Both dorsal fins are dusky coloured and other fins have a yellow tinge or are yellow. Very small dark or black spots are often found on the upper half of the body. The brassy tinge to the overall body colour gives rise to the common name. This species grows to around 80 cm, while the giant trevally can reach 1.7 metres.

TREVALLY, GIANT

Scientific name: Caranx ignobilis.
Also known as Lowly trevally, barrier trevally.

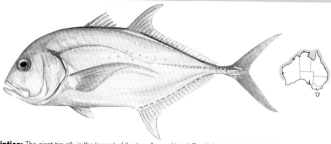

Description: The giant trevally is the largest of the trevally reaching 1.7 m in length and 60 kg which would be almost unstoppable on stand up fishing tackle. The steep profile of the head is typical of the giant trevally. There is also a small scale-less area on the ventral surface immediately in front of the ventral fins. A small patch of scales is generally found in the middle of this otherwise scale-less patch. There is no opercular (cheek) spot which is present on the bigeye trevally. As giant trevally increase in size, they form smaller schools with the largest fish frequently loners. Large fish also prefer deeper channels between large reefs while smaller fish are found on tidal flats or on the edges of shallower reefs.

Fishing: Small giant trevally are one of the most challenging species for lure fishers in the tropics, with spinning near the edges of reefs, on drop-offs on tidal flats or sight fishing to individuals or small schools working well. Poppers are particularly attractive to these fish and can also be used as a teaser for fly fishers. Giant trevally also take minnow lures, large spoons and lead-headed jigs. Large giant trevally are most frequently taken on live baits. They will also take dead baits, including fresh dead baits, cut baits, pilchards or less frequently squid or large prawn baits. Giant trevally can be hooked when bottom bouncing with standard reef rigs for other species such as coral trout or various emperors, with arm stretching and tackle testing results. Top quality gear and gel spun lines are an advantage in landing these challenging fish. Small giant trevally are good eating but fish over 10 – 12 kg are poor tasting and are better released after a photograph to record the encounter.

Rigs and Tactics:

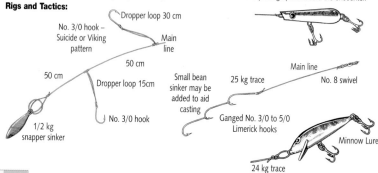

No. 3/0 hook –
Suicide or Viking
pattern

Dropper loop 30 cm

Main
line

50 cm

50 cm

Dropper loop 15cm

1/2 kg
snapper sinker

No. 3/0 hook

Small bean
sinker may be
added to aid
casting

25 kg trace

Ganged No. 3/0 to 5/0
Limerick hooks

Main line

No. 8 swivel

Minnow Lure

24 kg trace

TREVALLY, GOLDEN

Scientific name: Gnathanodon speciosus.

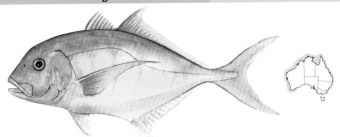

Description: The golden trevally is also a large species reaching 1.2 m and 37 kilograms. Juvenile golden trevally are striking and are often associated with large fish or sharks. They are a bright gold with vertical black stripes the first of which passes through the eye. Larger fish lose the distinctive stripes and the eye is quite small. These fish are often quite silvery when caught but flash yellow as they die and then are golden coloured, especially on the belly. A number of black spots are often present on the side, commonly near the tail but the number and size varies and they may not be present. The most obvious feature of this species is that they lack teeth.

TREVALLY, SILVER

Scientific name: Pseudocaranx dentex. Also known as White trevally, skipjack trevally, skippy.

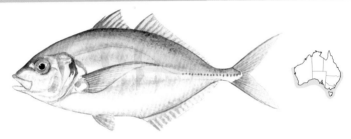

Description: A common schooling fish of cooler waters, the silver trevally is found in inshore areas but may be found near offshore cover. Juveniles are often encountered in estuaries and bays but larger fish can also be found in these areas on occasions. The fins may be yellow and a narrow yellow stripe is often found on these fish but most fish are silver with a blue-green or darker blue, and dark bands may be present. The silver trevally can reach 1 m and more than 10 kg but fish of 2 kg are much more common and in most areas, a fish of 5 kg is noteworthy. The mouth is relatively small, finishing well in front of the start of the eye and the lips are rubbery. There is an obvious black spot on the rear edge of the opercular (cheek) bone.

TURRUM

Scientific name: Carangoides fulvoguttatus.
Also known as Gold spotted trevally, yellow spotted trevally.

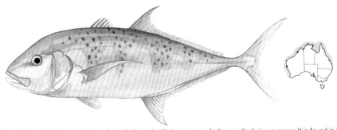

Description: The turrum is a largely tropical species that may move further south during summer. It is found in inshore waters and around shallow and occasionally mid water reefs. A number of species are known as turrum, especially in Queensland, but the true turrum can be identified by a number of features. These include the complete lack of scales up to the base of the pectoral fin whereas the giant trevally has a small oval shaped patch of tiny scales in an otherwise large scaleless area of the breast. The second dorsal fin of the turrum has between 25 – 30 rays while the giant trevally has 18 – 21. The turrum differs from many other trevally in only having a band of fine teeth in each jaw. The turrum can reach 1.3 m and a weight of around 12 kilograms.

TROUT COD

Scientific name: Maccullochella macquariensis.
Also known as Blue nose cod, bluenose, rock cod, blue cod.

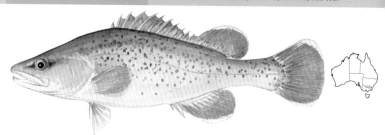

Description: The trout cod is capable of reaching 16 kg and 800 mm but much more common at 1 – 2 kilograms. A handsome aggressive fish which puts up a terrific fight for its size, the trout cod has a slate grey to greenish blue colour and dashed markings. Trout cod, particularly juveniles have a prominent stripe through the eye and an overhanging upper jaw. The tail wrist is much narrower than in Murray cod.

TROUT, RAINBOW

Scientific name: Oncorhynchus mykiss.
(formerly Salmo gairdnerii)
Also known as rainbow, 'bow, Steelhead.

Description: Rainbow trout possess the fleshy adipose fin of all salmonids behind the dorsal fin. The tail may be slightly forked but characteristically rainbow trout have spots over the entire tail and all of the body except the belly. A pink stripe along the body ranges from very pale in sea run and lake fish to crimson in river fish and those on their spawning run. Male rainbows develop a hooked lower jaw as spawning approaches. Females retain a more rounded head.

Fishing: Rainbow trout are generally easier to catch than brown trout but usually fight harder and often jump spectacularly. Rainbow trout are more mobile and will feed more freely in mid to shallow depths. This means that methods such as trolling are more successful, but rainbow trout can selectively feed on daphnia (water fleas) which can make them more difficult to catch.

Rainbow trout prefer faster water in streams than brown trout and will often take up station at the head of pools. Rainbow trout can be taken on fly, lure or bait. They take dry flies, wets, nymphs and streamer flies. Rainbow trout can be taken on bright colours and gaudy streamer flies can work well. Rainbow trout take all baits. A lightly weighted worm in streams or fairly close to the bank takes fish as do mudeyes fished under a bubble float or trolled with Cowbell trolling blades. Yabbies, grubs and live fish (where legal) take good catches.

Rigs and Tactics:

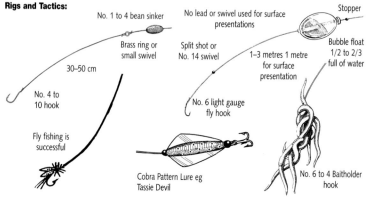

No. 1 to 4 bean sinker

Brass ring or small swivel

30–50 cm

No. 4 to 10 hook

Fly fishing is successful

No lead or swivel used for surface presentations

Split shot or No. 14 swivel

1–3 metres 1 metre for surface presentation

No. 6 light gauge fly hook

Cobra Pattern Lure eg Tassie Devil

Stopper

Bubble float 1/2 to 2/3 full of water

No. 6 to 4 Baitholder hook

TROUT, BROOK

Scientific name: Salvelinus fontinalis.
Also known as Brookie, brook char, char.

Description: The brook trout is a stunningly attractive species. The ventral and anal fins are bright orange with a black line and then a white leading edge. The markings on the dark upper body are either dots or irregular small lines of cream or off white. The dorsal fin has wavy colouration.

The males in spawning condition develop a markedly hooked jaw and even brighter colours. The mouth is large, extending well behind the back edge of the eye. The tail is large and moderately indented or lightly forked.

The brook trout can reach around 4 kg in Australia, but the largest fish are generally released brood stock from the hatcheries. These fish do extremely well in hatcheries but do not adapt nearly as well to the wild, except in Lake Jindabyne. Any wild caught brook trout is a prize in Australia.

TROUT, BROWN

Scientific name: Salmo trutta.
Also known as Brownie, sea trout, Loch Leven trout.

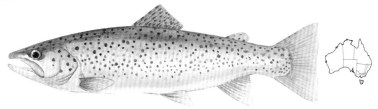

Description: The brown trout is a handsome fish which can exhibit wide colour variations, partly dependent upon the environment in which the fish is found. Sea run fish and some lake dwelling fish are silver in colour with a few spots on the body. River fish in particular can have a beautiful golden sheen and large black spots on the upper body. There are frequently beautiful red spots, surrounded by a white halo below the lateral line which may be mixed with black spots. In all fish, the dorsal fins have some spots but the tail fin has none or a few very faint spots. The tail fin is either square or very slightly indented, whereas the Atlantic salmon has an obvious indent or fork to the tail. The adipose fin is obvious and may be lobe-like in larger fish. The mouth is large and the jaws become hooked to a degree in males during spawning. The brown trout can reach 25 kg overseas, but in Australia they have been recorded to 14 kilograms.

Fishing: Brown trout are generally the most highly regarded Australian trout species, due to their large size and the skill which is needed to entice these fish to strike. Brown trout take a variety of foods which may include other trout, minnows, insect larvae, terrestrial insects, snails and worms. Brown trout can be taken throughout the day, but the best times are dawn, dusk and at night. Night time is often the best in heavily fished waters, where a few wily, large, and often cannibalistic specimens can often be found. Many brown trout are taken on fly, with nymphs, streamers, wet flies and dry flies all taking fish. Many brown trout feed heavily on yabbies or snails and imitations of these can be very productive. Brown trout generally prefer the slower waters of pools or the tails of pools in streams or deeper waters of lakes, moving into feeding stations during peak periods. Brown trout are also taken on a wide variety of lures, with favourites including lead head jigs, spoons, bladed lures like the Celta, and minnow or yabby lures. Brown trout take a variety of baits, with mudeyes, yabbies, minnows, grubs and worms being most successful. Brown trout will also take maggots, garden snails, corn, cheese, marshmallows and dog food on at least some occasions.

Rigs and Tactics:

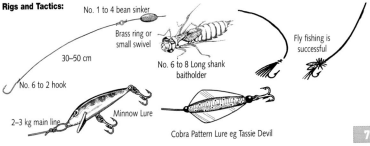

No. 1 to 4 bean sinker

Brass ring or
small swivel

30–50 cm

No. 6 to 2 hook

2–3 kg main line

No. 6 to 8 Long shank
baitholder

Minnow Lure

Fly fishing is
successful

Cobra Pattern Lure eg Tassie Devil

TROUT, CORAL

Scientific name: Plectropomus leopardus. Also known as Leopard cod, leopard trout, trout, blue-spot trout.

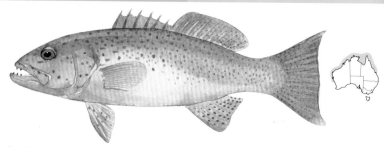

Description: The coral trout is frequently confused with other similar species, but the coral trout has numerous small and always round spots on the head and body. The colour varies but can be a brilliant red or red-orange or a brick red. The soft dorsal fin is rounded and the tail square cut which may have a blue edge. It has a large mouth and sharp but widely spaced canine teeth. The coral trout grows to over a metre and 20 kg, but can be over fished and is generally taken at a smaller size. Irresponsible overfishing for the live fish export trade in Queensland has had a big impact on coral trout numbers there.

Fishing: This is undoubtedly one of the premier reef fish due to its brilliant appearance, hard fight near coral outcrops and excellent eating. Coral trout can be taken on bait, lure and fly but fishing is typified by a short battle of strength and will between the angler and the coral trout. Best lures include minnow lures which dive to different depths, as coral trout will readily move upwards to slam a lure. Poppers can take some large fish. Coral trout, like many of the cod which are found in similar areas, can take large baits, with live baits being best, followed by whole dead fish, fresh fillets, pilchards, prawns and squid. A trace can offer some protection during the fight. The frequent presence of numerous sharp coral outcrops in many locations and a strong fish like the coral trout means that if the fish is given his head a break-off is certain. Some of the largest coral trout are taken in deeper waters near less obvious cover, providing a welcome surprise for the lucky angler. Large coral trout have been implicated with ciguatera and some caution should be exercised with the largest fish, consuming a small portion initially otherwise this species provides a culinary delight.

Rigs and Tactics:

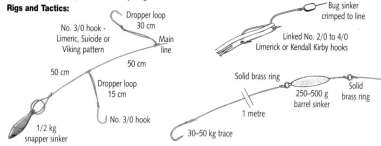

TOADFISH, COMMON

Scientific name: Tetractenos hamiltoni. Also known as blowie, toado

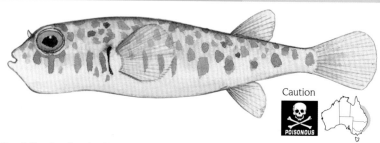

Caution

POISONOUS

Description: A small species of the toadfish reaching only 15 centimetes. The body is fairly slender and there are several vertical stripes on the lower sides of the body. There is no long stripe along the body as in the banded toadfish. The common toadfish also has small prickles over its skin whereas the smooth toadfish has smooth skin. Like all the toadfish, the common toadfish will inflate its body with air or water upon capture which makes the prickles stand up. Although much despised, the toadfish are one of the most advanced groups of fish from an evolutionary standpoint, a feature which is generally lost on those who catch them regularly.

TROUT, CORONATION

Scientific name: Variola louti.
Also known as Lunar-tailed cod, fairy cod.

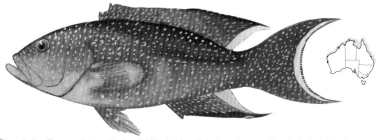

Description: The coronation trout is a beautiful fish which has vivid red or red-orange colouration flecked with yellow or red. The tail is distinctive with a sickle or lunar crescent shape and a distinctive yellow trailing edge. The cheeks and all the other fins are tinged with yellow on the trailing edge. The coronation trout is quite common on coral reefs, but may be found on deeper reefs to 100 metres. It grows to 80 cm and around 3 kilograms.

Fishing: The coronation trout shares many features from an angling perspective with the coral trout, including a large mouth, aggressive nature, a strong lure taker and excellent eating. They can have tapeworms in the guts which do not affect the eating quality of the fish. Coronation trout can be taken on minnows, jigs and chrome lures and flies. Live baits, dead baits and cut baits work best. A trace is an advantage, especially as coral trout can be taken from the same areas. As the coronation trout will move upwards to take a bait, less weight is necessary and a mobile approach, casting or drifting with the tide on reef edges or channels works well. The fight is strong, but the fish are not as big as coral trout.

Rigs and Tactics:

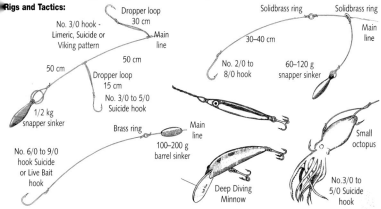

TREVALLY, BIGEYE

Scientific name: Caranx sexfasciatus.
Also known as Great trevally.

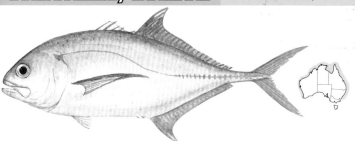

Description: Positive identification of all trevally species is particularly difficult. The bigeye trevally is best identified by the gelatinous covering to the rear of the relatively large eye. There are white tips to the dorsal and anal fins and a small black spot on the rear edge of the gill cover. The bigeye trevally's breast is fully scaled which separates it from the giant trevally. The soft dorsal fin of the bigeye trevally has 19 – 22 soft rays while the turrum, with which it is sometimes confused has 25 – 30 rays. Juvenile bigeye trevally prefer the tidal flats and can be quite common while larger fish patrol close to deep drop-offs especially those close to high tidal flows or near reef gaps. This is not a large species, reaching only 80 centmetres.

TROUT, BAR-CHEEKED CORAL

Scientific name: Plectropomus maculatus. Also known as Bar-cheeked trout, coral cod.

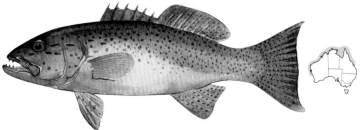

Description: The bar-cheeked coral trout can be as brilliantly coloured as the coral trout with which it is often confused. The bar-cheek coral trout is most easily separated by the blue spots on the head being elongated and not round as they are in coral trout. This species is smaller than the coral trout, reaching 70 cm and 6 kg but can be susceptible to overfishing and is generally taken at a smaller size. Almost all coral trout taken in WA are this species. The bar-cheek coral trout has the same powerful tail which is used to good effect to bury anglers in reef country. It has a large mouth and sharp but widely spaced canine teeth.

Fishing: One of the premier reef fish due to its brilliant appearance, hard fight near coral outcrops and excellent eating. The bar-cheek coral trout can be taken on bait, lure and fly. Trolled minnow lures and cast poppers, slices or jigs put near coral outcrops or channels between reefs can provide exciting sport. The proximity of sharp coral outcrops in many locations means that if the fish is given his head a break-off is certain. Quality tackle and close attention, especially when trolling is required. The larger fish can be taken in deeper water. The bar-cheek coral trout can take large baits. Best baits are live baits, with whole fish and fresh fillets working well, and squid, prawn and crab taking fish. A trace can offer some protection during the fight. This species makes excellent eating.

Rigs and Tactics:

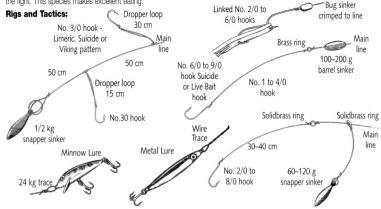

TRUMPETER

Scientific name: Pelates quadrilineatus.
Also known as four-lined trumpeter.

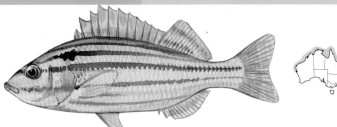

Description: A common bait stealing species of the estuaries and coastal bays. While it has a wide range, it is best known from NSW where it forms schools over weed and sand areas from the Sydney region northwards and disrupts bream, whiting and flathead fishing. The trumpeter has a more elongated nose than the striped trumpeter and there are four or five prominent stripes which run the length of the body. The mouth is relatively small, and as it only grows to 20 cm, this species is difficult to hook. A dark blotch behind the head and under the start of the dorsal fin is usually present.

TRUMPETER, STRIPED

Scientific name: Pelates sexlineatus. Also known as Striped perch, striped grunter, trump.

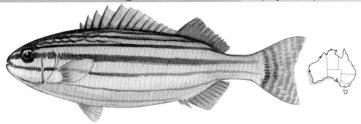

Description: A small species reaching 32 cm and around 500 g, but more common at a bait stealing 25 centimetres. The striped trumpeter forms schools in coastal bays and estuaries over sand or weed bottom or near broken ground. The small mouth makes hooking difficult. The short head is quite rounded and there are around 5 – 6 lines running through the head and along the body. There may be a number of vertical blotches with one most prominent behind the head overlaying the stripes. The top stripes may be wavy.

Fishing: While frequently considered a pest species, the striped trumpeter is a frequent early encounter for young anglers. The striped trumpeter will take most baits, but the small mouth means that a small long-shanked hook will improve catches. Baits of peeled prawns, cut flesh, blue bait, pipi, worms, or squid work well, with more robust baits such as squid recommended. Striped trumpeter make hardy and quality live baits. Striped trumpeter are not highly regarded as food fish but are often served to the family by proud young fishermen.

Rigs and Tactics:

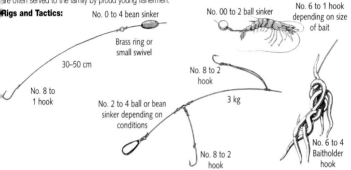

TRUMPETER, TASMANIAN

Scientific name: Latris lineata.

Also known as Striped trumpeter, common trumpeter, stripey, real trumpeter.

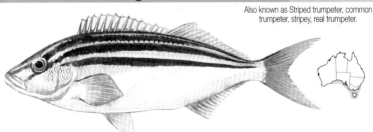

Description: The Tamanian trumpeter is is a medium to large species reaching 1.2 m and up to 25 kg, although the largest fish are found in deep waters. Overfishing has depleted stocks of the Tasmanian trumpeter on inshore reefs, where mainly juveniles are now found. The Tasmanian trumpeter has three distinctive brownish stripes along the sides. The Tasmanian trumpeter is easily separated from the similar morwongs as it lacks the extended 'fingers' on the pectoral fins. The fins are dusky and may have a yellow or reddish tinge. The mouth is large and the lips quite blubbery.

Fishing: Fishing is with standard deep reef fishing rigs, with sufficient weight to get the bait to the bottom. Best baits are squid, prawns, octopus or cut fish baits. Pilchards and other small whole fish or live baits will also work well. Tasmanian trumpeter are occasionally taken on large lead head or vertical jigs, but tipping with squid increases strike rates. Smaller fish are likely to be encountered on inshore reefs and like many reef species, the smaller the size of the fish, the larger the school is likely to be. Working the edges of reefs when a school is located will bring good catches. The Tasmanian trumpeter is excellent eating and is rated as one of the best cool water reef species.

TRUMPETER, BASTARD

Scientific name: Latridopsis forsteri. Also known as Moki, copper moki, silver trumpeter.

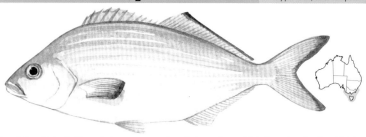

Description: The bastard trumpeter is a common species on inshore reefs especially in Tasmania and southern Victoria. This species can reach 65 cm and more than 4 kilograms. In smaller sizes, it forms schools but larger specimens are more solitary and can be found in waters beyond 30 fathoms. The mouth is small and set low down. The back and upper flanks are silvery-brown with a pattern of close-set slender yellow or white lines running along the body. The fins are brownish in colour and the edges of the pectoral, dorsal and the forked tail fin are black.

Fishing: The bastard trumpeter is occasionally taken by anglers on baits of prawn, squid, cockles or worms. The small mouth means that a smaller, long-shanked hook will increase catches, as will berley. Standard snapper rigs with smaller hooks will take this fish. The bastard trumpeter is more frequently taken by spearfishermen. The bastard trumpeter is excellent eating.

Rigs and Tactics:

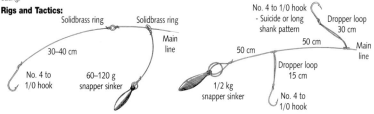

TUNA, MACKEREL

Scientific name: Euthynnus affinis. Also known as Jack mackerel, little tuna, kawa-kawa.

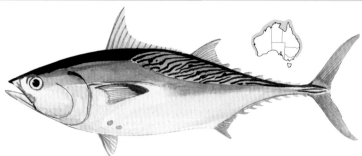

Description: The mackerel tuna is a highly prized lightweight game species which is caught in inshore waters or larger bays, harbours and large estuarine systems as well as around offshore islands or larger reefs. The mackerel tuna can reach 1 m in length and 12 kg but is much more common at 2 – 8 kilograms.

The mackerel tuna has prominent wavy green lines in the rear portion of the body above the midline. The mackerel tuna is similar to the frigate mackerel but the first dorsal of the mackerel tuna reaches almost to the second dorsal while the frigate mackerel's first dorsal is short and widely separated from the second dorsal fin. The mackerel tuna has two to five dark spots above the ventral fin and more prominent teeth than the frigate mackerel which also only reaches 58 cm in length.

Fishing: The mackerel tuna is a schooling fish which feeds heavily on pilchards, herrings, whitebait, anchovies, squid and occasionally krill. However, even when a feeding school is located, they can be very selective and difficult to entice to strike.

Mackerel tuna are mainly taken on fast trolled or high speed retrieved lures such as plastic skirted lures, Christmas tree lures, minnow lures, plastic squids, lead jigs and feather lures and spoons. The mackerel tuna will take live baits, fresh dead baits either cast and retrieved, trolled or fished under a float. They will more rarely take cut baits. Mackerel tuna are a frequent catch of high speed land based game fishermen.

TUNA, LONGTAIL

Scientific name: Thunnus tonggol.
Also known as Northern bluefin tuna, northern blue.

Description: The name longtail comes from the light build to the rear half of this species, giving a narrow tail wrist and a slender outline. The pectoral fin is very short and finishes well in front of the start of the second dorsal fin which readily separates the species from yellowfin and bigeye tuna. This species is much more common in tropical waters but can migrate southwards in summer.

Fishing: In tropical waters, small longtails can form vast schools like mackerel tuna or bonito. These schools move rapidly and fish can be caught by casting lures or trolling lures or baits near the edge of the feeding school. Minnow lures, lead slugs or Christmas tree lures, feather jigs, spoons and flies all work well with larger fish preferring larger lures and a faster retrieve.

Longtail prefer inshore waters and although most are taken by anglers in boats, longtail are a highly prized land based game species. Specialised gear with live baits below large floats or balloons or high speed spinning can bring these speedsters to the rocks. As with all rock based fishing, special care should be taken of wave conditions, especially when landing large fish.

Longtail love live baits fished from boats and cubing (berleying with tuna flesh and feeding unweighted cubes into the trail, one with a hook) can work well once a school is located.

Longtail tuna are red fleshed and of lower quality than many species, but it is greatly improved with immediate bleeding.

Rigs and Tactics:

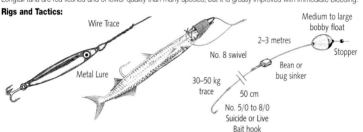

TUNA, BIGEYE

Scientific name: Thunnus obesus.

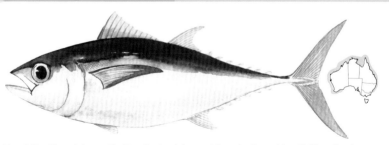

Description: The eye is large and the bigeye tuna is quite heavy set. The anal and second dorsal fin lobes, although elongated are not obviously extended. The pectoral fin extends to the commencement of the second dorsal lobe which readily separates this species from the bluefins with shorter pectoral fins and the albacore with its extremely long pectoral fin.

Small bigeye tuna are often confused with small yellowfin tuna which do not have the obvious sickle-like anal and second dorsal fins. In small bigeye tuna the eye is larger, the liver is prominently striated (with ridges and grooves) and they do not have whitish bars across the body.

A prominent keel near the tail base is located between two smaller keels with the bigeye.

The bigeye favours offshore waters and is commonly taken by longlining off the Continental Shelf, although juveniles can be taken in inshore waters. It can reach 2.35 m in length and nearly 200 kg, but Australian specimens are generally smaller than 40 – 50 kilograms.

TUNA, SOUTHERN BLUEFIN

Scientific name:
Thunnus maccoyii.

Also known as SBT, southern blue, bluefin, bluey, tunny.

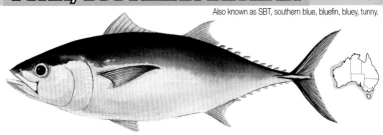

Description: The southern bluefin tuna is a heavily built and very highly prized species which prefers open oceanic waters, especially in larger sizes. The southern bluefin tuna can grow to greater than 150 kg but is most commonly caught well below this size. Small southern bluefin can be found in inshore waters and weigh from 3 – 25 kg, with the average size generally increasing as you move eastwards along the southern coast. Southern bluefin tuna have been overexploited by commercial fishing operations, especially on the high seas. The commercial overexploitation has lead to the development of extensive aquaculture, based around Port Lincoln to on-grow these fish; a process which previously occurred naturally before overfishing of juveniles removed larger adults from the south-east. Southern bluefin tuna can be identified by their heavy bodies, and the short pectoral fins which do not extend to the second dorsal. The dorsal and anal lobes are also short as opposed to the yellowfin with its scythe-like lobes in larger fish. The finlets at the rear of the body are edged with black and the caudal keels on the wrist of the tail are conspicuously yellow, especially in the sizes normally encountered by recreational fishers.

Fishing: Most southern bluefin tuna are taken on trolled lures, with rubber squids, pushers and other gamefishing lures working well. They will also take minnow lures, feathers, slices and large lead slugs. Southern bluefin tuna like offshore debris and can be taken around floating logs, shipping containers or other large flotsam in bluewater areas. Southern bluefin tuna are less frequently taken on baits, although they can be taken on trolled baits, live baits or dead baits including cubes, especially if used with berley. Deep fished live baits or whole squid can take larger fish, but local knowledge is necessary. The southern bluefin tuna has rich dark meat which is highly prized for sashimi.

TUNA, STRIPED

Scientific name: Katsuwonis pelamis.
Also known as Skipjack, skipjack tuna, stripey, aku.

Description: The striped tuna is a small, thickset schooling species which rapidly tapers at the rear of the body to a smallish tail. Sometimes misidentified as a bonito, but striped tuna lack the obvious teeth of the bonito and have no stripes on the upper flanks or back. Instead, the 4 – 6 horizontal stripes on the striped tuna are found on the lower flanks and belly. The area under and around the pectoral fin lacks stripes. The striped tuna can reach more than 15 kg, but in Australia any fish over 10 kg is exceptional and the average size is between 1 and 6 kilograms. Schools of striped tuna can be massive and may contain hundreds of tonnes of fish. This species forms the basis of significant commercial fisheries in many countries.

Fishing: Striped tuna are mainly taken on lures trolled or cast from boats, deep shores or jetties which extend to deeper water. Many striped tuna are taken on heavy cord lines and Smiths jigs to be used as bait or berley. Striped tuna provide excellent sport on lighter lines as they are very hard fighting speedsters.

Most bright lures which work well at around 5 knots will take striped tuna, with Christmas tree style lures working well. Slices, slug lures, feather jigs, small poppers and medium sized flies also take good numbers of fish, although striped tuna can be finicky about size and action type of lures at times.

Striped tuna can be taken on pilchards, cut baits or squid, especially if a berley trail excites the fish. Larger fish can take small live baits. Striped tuna have very dark red meat which is quite strongly flavoured but is suitable for smoking, salting and canning. If bled and chilled immediately they are fair eating. However, striped tuna are excellent live baits for large pelagics and their cut flesh makes a first rate bait or berley where their oil rich red flesh attracts most species.

TUNA, YELLOWFIN

Scientific name: Thunnus albacares.
Also known as Allison tuna, yellowfin or 'fin, ahi.

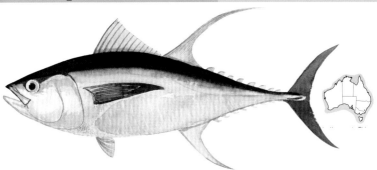

Description: The yellowfin tuna is a beautiful, powerful and challenging sportsfish which prefers warmer currents but may move inshore where deep water comes close to the coast. The yellowfin tuna is easily separated from other tunas by the scythe-like dorsal and anal lobes in adult fish. The pectoral fin is long and extends to the commencement of the second dorsal fin.

Small yellowfin have short dorsal and anal lobes, but have whitish bars down the sides which may disappear after death. The liver of yellowfin tuna is smooth as opposed to the ridged liver of the bigeye. The caudal keels (ridges) on the wrist of the tail are also dusky and never yellow as in the southern bluefin tuna.

Yellowfin tuna can reach more than 200 kg in other parts of the world, but in Australia fish over 100 kg are magnificent and most fish are between 2 and 50 kilograms.

Rigs and Tactics:

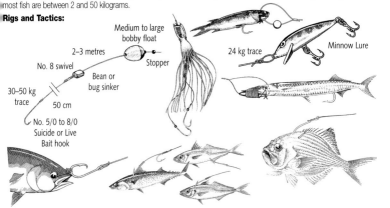

TUSKFISH, VENUS

Scientific name: Choerodon venustus.
Also known as Cockie.

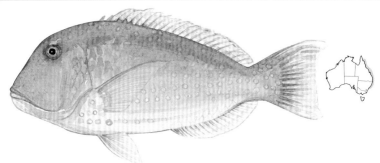

Description: The venus tuskfish is a fairly small species, reaching 5 kg but most commonly seen at around a kilogram. They are generally bright pink along the flanks, being darker above and paler on the belly. There are numerous small white or blue spots on the body and the fins and tail are splashed with blue as are the lips and chin. The venus tuskfish prefers shallow to mid depth reef country and is found very close to reefs where it feeds.

TUSKFISH, BLACK-SPOT

Scientific name: Choerodon schoenleinii. Also known as Blue parrot.

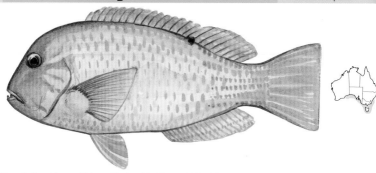

Description: A large tuskfish capable of reaching 15 kg and is found in sand and weed areas adjacent to coral reefs. The black-spot tuskfish is easily identified by the black spot which is found at the base of the middle of the dorsal fin. There is often a short, oblique purple bar set behind the eye and the tail is generally bright purple. The overall body colour is generally blue and is blue-green or purple whereas in the blue tuskfish (Choerodon cyanodus) which is a smaller species, the chin is white or off-white.

Fishing: The black-spot tuskfish has a strong preference for crab baits but can be taken on prawns, squid, pipi and worms. The black-spot tusk fish can often be observed and cast to, making presentation with lightly weighted baits less difficult, but they can be difficult to entice to strike on occasion. Because this species can move close inshore to graze on corals in a quest for larger food, they can be taken by spearfishermen. The black-spot tuskfish can be caught near deeper reefs where lightly fished and larger specimens are more likely. The black-spot tuskfish can be a challenging capture as they can cut off the unwary on nearby coral outcrops and is not easily brought to the boat. The black-spot tuskfish is excellent eating with firm white flesh.

Rigs and Tactics:

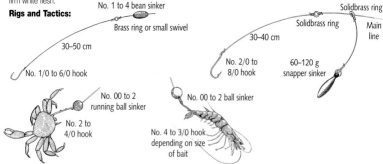

No. 1 to 4 bean sinker

Brass ring or small swivel

30–50 cm

No. 1/0 to 6/0 hook

Solidbrass ring

Solidbrass ring

Main line

30–40 cm

No. 2/0 to 8/0 hook

60–120 g snapper sinker

No. 00 to 2 running ball sinker

No. 2 to 4/0 hook

No. 00 to 2 ball sinker

No. 4 to 3/0 hook depending on size of bait

WAHOO

Scientific name: Acanthocybium solandri. Also known as Ono, 'hoo.

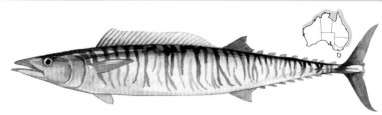

Description: The wahoo is a long and sleek pelagic species which is capable of very fast movement in the water. Most wahoo in Australian waters are between 8 and 30 kg but they can reach 65 kilograms. The wahoo is a solitary open water species which can be identified by the long and higher dorsal fin of approximately even height. The dorsal fin starts behind the commencement of the pectoral fin while with the Spanish mackerel it commences at the leading edge of the pectoral. The head is longer and more pointed with the wahoo and the trailing edge of the tail fin is vertical compared to the forked tail of the other mackerels. The wahoo has a number of prominent zebra-like vertical stripes along the body but these are less noticeable in some especially larger specimens and fade considerably after death.

WAREHOU

Scientific name: Seriolella brama. Also known as Silver warehou, blue warehou, snotty trevally, snot-nose trevalla, snot-gall, snotty.

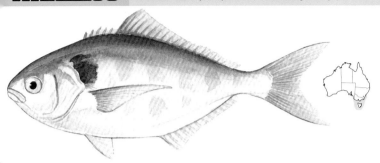

Description: The warehou is a deep water schooling reef fish that can make inshore migrations, especially during winter. The warehou is especially common in Tasmanian and Victorian waters. The warehou grows to 7 kg with smaller specimens more likely to be encountered in the shallower waters more commonly fished by recreational anglers. The warehou is best identified by the rounded head and the dark patch behind the head and above the pectoral fin, but this fades with death. Warehou look similar to silver trevally but lack the scutes along the side near the tail. The warehou has a thick mucous coating and translucent nose area which gives rise to its less appetising common names like snotty.

WHITING, GRASS

Scientific name: Haletta semifasciata. Also known as Rock whiting, blue rock whiting, weed whiting, stranger.

Description: Although the grass whiting vaguely resembles other whitings, this species is more closely related to the wrasses or parrotfish as it possesses fused teeth. It is a relatively common species which prefers seagrass habitats but may be found on nearby sand patches or shallow reefs. There is a single long dorsal fin compared with two dorsal fins for whiting. The grass whiting can reach 41 centimetres. There is vastly different colouring between males and females, with males a brighter bluish green with a black blotch towards the rear of the dorsal fin. Females and juveniles have pale greenish-brown backs which fade to brown after death. There is a distinctive blue blotch around the anus.

WHITING, SAND

Scientific name: Sillago ciliata. Also known as Silver whiting, summer whiting, blue nose whiting.

Description: The sand whiting is a common species of inshore and tidal sandy areas. The sand whiting can reach 47 cm and around a kilogram. It is readily identified by the lack of a silver stripe along the side and the dusky blotch at the base of the pectoral fin. Large sand whiting are sometimes confused with bonefish, but all whitings have two dorsal fins while the bonefish has one.

Fishing: The sand whiting feeds on nippers, pipis, prawns and especially beach, squirt or blood worms and all these make terrific baits. On a rising tide, sand whiting can be caught in very shallow water of only a few centimetres, while on a falling tide, fish the deeper edges of gutters or drop-offs but success is less assured.

WHITING, KING GEORGE

Scientific name: Sillaginodes punctata. Also known as Spotted whiting, KG, KGW.

Description: The King George whiting is the largest and most sought after whiting species in Australia reaching 67 cm and more than 2 kg, with the largest specimens found in oceanic waters. Juveniles spend time near sea grass beds inshore or in estuaries before moving to more open waters. King George whiting prefer sand patches near weed beds, gravel or broken reef country. King George whiting are readily identified by the distinctive dark brown or red-brown spots and broken dashes along the body.

Fishing: The King George whiting is a magnificent and hard fighting whiting species. Smaller fish succumb most readily to baits of prawn, pipi, mussel, and worms. These baits are fished on light line with minimal weight near the edges of drop-offs or sand patches in sea grass beds or reef areas. Larger fish are often caught on blue sardines or whitebait. The largest King George whiting are taken on reef fishing rigs near reefs in depths up to 30 metres. The best King George whiting experts adopt a mobile approach, fishing sand patches near heavy cover and moving on if there are no bites in a few minutes. The King George whiting is magnificent eating, combining the meat quality of all whiting in a size large enough that generous boneless fillets can be obtained.

Rigs and Tactics:

No. 6 to 1/0 hook

No. 2 to 4 ball or bean sinker depending on conditions

3 kg

No. 6 to 1/0 hook

No. 1 to 3 bean sinker

No. 2 to 1/0 hook

No. 2 to 5 ball sinker

20 cm dropper

40–50 cm dropper

No. 8 to 2 Long Shank, Eastern Estuary or Suicide hook depending on size of KGW sought

WHITING, YELLOWFIN

Scientific name: Sillago schombergki Also known as western sand whiting, yellow-finned whiting

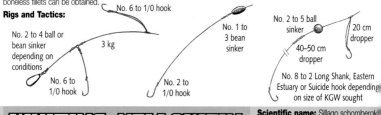

Description: A similar species to the sand whiting but lacks the black spot at the base of the pectoral fin. The characteristic yellow to orange ventral and anal fins become less apparent in larger individuals. There is no obvious silver strip along the sides or any markings on the dorsal surface. It is found in estuaries and surf areas and can reach 42 centimetres. It is not uncommon at around 33 – 35 centimetres.

Fishing: The excellent eating which this species provides makes it a worthwhile target for anglers. While they may be found in the estuaries, with the exception of the Peel-Harvey estuary, the best specimens are taken from ocean beaches. A light ball sinker and a bluebait or whitebait on small ganged hooks fished on a flick rod are highly recommended. When fishing for whiting, fishing at your feet first is good advice as many anglers cast way out behind the active feeding zone of this fish. They fish much better on a rising tide and can be in the sand wash area in only a few centimetres of water. A slow retrieve works best.

Rigs and Tactics:

No. 8 to 4 long shank hook

No. 1 to 3 bean sinker

No. 2 bug sinker

No. 6 to 2 linked Limerick hooks

No. 00 to 1 ball sinker

No. 6 to 4 light gauge fly hook

WHITING, SOUTHERN SCHOOL

Scientific name: Sillago bassensis
Also known as silver whiting

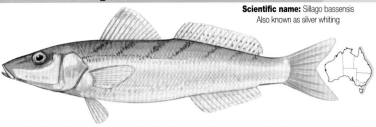

Description: The whitings can be extremely difficult to tell apart and the southern school whiting is one of the more difficult species to separate. The eastern school whiting (Sillago flindersi) only overlaps its range in Western Port in Victoria and is more heavily marked on the dorsal surface. The bars or streaks on the top of the southern school whiting may be very faint and a light orange or sandy brown colour. Under the water these streaks are very difficult to see. After death these bars may fade entirely giving a silver appearance. There is no spot at the base of the pectoral fin which separates the southern school whiting from all other similar species other than the yellow-fin whiting which has yellow to orange ventral fins. The southern school whiting is found on inshore sandy areas and will follow the tide onto sand flats and beaches. Although they are taken by recreational fishers in shallow waters, they can be taken on deeper sand bank and are trawled by commercial fishers to a depth of 55 metres. The southern school whiting can reach a very pleasing 36 centimetres.

WHITING, TRUMPETER

Scientific name: Sillago maculata.
Also known as Diver whiting, winter whiting, spotted whiting.

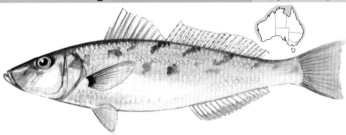

Description: The trumpeter whiting is a common schooling fish with a preference for silty bottom or deeper gutters of bays and estuaries. The trumpeter whiting is more commonly taken during the cooler months, especially on the east coast. The trumpeter whiting reaches 30 centimetres.

It is easily identified by having a series of irregular and disjointed brown blotches, spots or vertical marks. The similar eastern school whiting (Sillago flindersi) or southern school whiting (Sillago bassensis) both have unbroken vertical stripes. All of these species have a silver stripe which runs along the middle of the body.

WIRRAH

Scientific name: Acanthistius ocellatus.
Also known as Eastern wirrah, wirrah cod, peppermint cod, meat wirrah, boot.

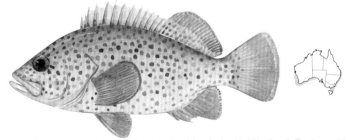

Description: The wirrah is common on exposed coastal reefs with juveniles found in tidal rock pools. The characteristic spots over the head and body of the wirrah are blue in the centre. There are 13 spines in the first dorsal fin and the fins are edged by blue-grey. The wirrah can reach 64 cm in length.

Fishing: A large mouth makes this species easy prey for kids dangling baited hooks into rock pools. Wirrah will feed readily on most baits, preferring fresh cut baits, prawns, pilchard or virtually anything they can fit into their mouths. The wirrah is not targeted by serious anglers.

The flesh is coarse, tough and flavourless, making the wirrah a 'mother-in-law' fish.

WRASSE, MAORI

Scientific name: Opthalmolepis lineolatus.
Also known as southern Maori wrasse, Maori

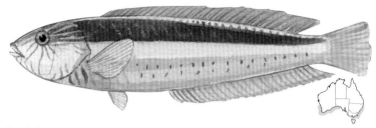

Description: An attractive wrasse which can reach 41 cm, but is more often encountered at a smaller, bait stealing size. This species is found on inshore, or more often offshore reefs throughout its range. The males and females are different in appearance. The males have a black stripe along the body below the mid line. While both sexes have a prominent orange brown top to the body, the male has a number of bright blue spots through this area. Both male and female Maori wrasse have a number of small blue stripes on the head. The belly is yellow or creamy yellow and is below a wide white stripe down the side of the fish.

Fishing: The small mouth of this species and the fact that it occupies a similar area to more highly valued reef species such as snapper, morwong and dhufish means that the Maori wrasse is not highly regarded by anglers. The Maori wrasse can be taken on most baits, including on bait jigs when they are on inshore bait grounds. The Maori wrasse is generally used as a cut bait, but they make a quite acceptable live bait, being hardy and attractive to fish like Samson fish, kingfish and big snapper. The Maori wrasse is not generally targeted but is taken on standard reef fishing rigs. It is not generally regarded as a food fish but makes quite acceptable eating.

YELLOWTAIL

Scientific name: Trahurus novaezelandiae.
Also known as Yellowtail scad, scad, yakka, bung, chow.

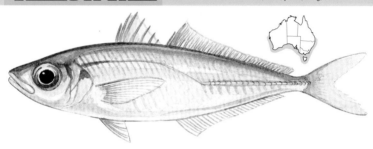

Description: The yellowtail is a common schooling forage fish of inshore estuaries, bays or inshore oceanic waters. The yellowtail reaches 33 cm but is most commonly encountered at between 18 and 25 centimetres. Larger fish are almost certainly cowanyoung (also called horse mackerel or jack mackerel Trachurus declivis). Yellowtail have scutes (large scales along the lateral line) which extend from the back of the head whereas similar southern mackerel-scad (Decapterus muroadsi) or Russell mackerel-scad (Decapterus russelli) only have scutes at the rear of the body.

Fishing: Gear can be as basic as a handline with 4 kg line and a size 12 long-shanked hook. One or no split shot completes the rig. Yellowtail will take most baits, but the most common baits are small pieces of cut bait, prawn, squid, mince meat, heart or mullet roe. Yellowtail respond very well to berley, with bran, pollard or commercial berleys working well. Many yellowtail are now taken on commercial bait jigs, either fished lightly weighted or vertically jigged with a larger sinker, but there are restrictions on the number of hooks in most states. Yellowtail make very good whole dead baits with fairly oily flesh, but they are arguably the best live bait available. The common name yakka comes from the work that yellowtail put in as a very hardy live bait.

Yellowtail should be lightly hooked in the back and either fished under a float or drift fished for all manner of larger fish. Yellowtail make acceptable eating but there are a number of small bones.

CALAMARI, SOUTHERN

Scientific name: Sepioteuthis australis Also known as calamari, calamari squid, southern squid.

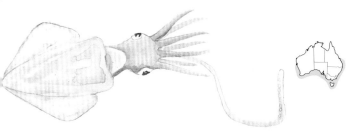

Description: A moderate sized and lightly framed squid with smooth skin that reaches up to 50 cm in length. The fins extend along the entire length of the body, forming a diamond shape. Like most squid, there are eight arms and two extendable feeding tentacles, however the arms and tips of the feeding tentacles have suckers with a horny teethed rim which can grip very well when handling the southern calamari. The colour patterns are generally yellow-green to orange but can vary rapidly while chasing bait, being handled or in a bucket of water. There are often three or four dark bars across the upper or lower surfaces of the body. The shell or 'pen' is almost transparent and quite thin as opposed to the heavy shell of the cuttlefish. The southern calamari is common in shallow inshore waters, often in sand habitats and seagrass meadows. It is more active at night but can also be regularly caught during the day. Smaller calamari form small schools and largest specimens tend to be solitary. They are attracted to lights. Their main defences are jetting away from danger and ink squirting but they also camouflage well amongst weed. The southern calamari can eject its ink quite a distance and always seems to have just that little bit left for when you try and unhook it. Most anglers allow the squid to squirt several times before bringing them on board, but boating a recently hooked squid on board as a way to repay family members who had cast aspersions on angling ability. The ink washes out and is prized as part of a pasta sauce.

Fishing: Calamari are one of the species that inspires celebration of Australia's multicultural history. Once despised or used solely as bait, many anglers target little else and rate them above many of the smaller finfish that are also found in similar areas. The southern calamari is delightful eating and fresh caught ones that are ringed and very quickly cooked in a batter of two parts flour and one part salt and one part pepper are divine. Southern calamari will take most fish baits and can be a nuisance, attacking live baits set for other species. They can be frustrating to hook on a gang hook rig, but a bait rigged on a squid jig will get you a quality feed. The special cloth covered squid jigs work extremely well and everyone has a favourite colour or pattern. A better quality squid jig will catch more squid. A slow jerky retrieve will work best. While a small live southern calamari makes an excellent bait and larger ones make a great bottom bait, this is a waste of such a great meal.

CUTTLEFISH

Scientific name: Sepia apama. Also known as giant cuttlefish, Australian cuttlefish

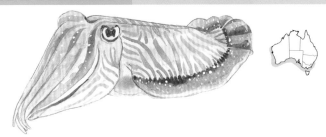

Description: The cuttlefish species most common in southern Australian waters is one of the world's largest species reaching 5 kilograms and 60 cm main body length. The cuttlefish is easily separated from other cephalopods because of the thickness and size of the shell. This shell is the cuttlebone which delights budgies the world over and is often found washed up on beaches after a storm. The cuttlefish feeds on small fish, crabs or prawns by shooting out two tentacles which are normally carried in small pouches near the eyes. The cuttlefish also possesses excellent camouflage. Cuttlefish can be found in depths of up to 50 metres and can move into inshore waters to breed, in winter, where they can be tracked by predatory fish such as snapper.

Fishing: Cuttlefish can be taken with squid jigs, but they are less commonly specifically targeted. They are also more easily taken on fish baits and can be an interesting by-catch when bottom bouncing in cooler waters. The cuttlefish possesses the same inking capability as the squids but when in jumbo sizes can eject lots of ink a long way - don't say you haven't been warned! The cuttlefish makes excellent bait but is slightly less highly regarded for food than the squid as large cuttlefish can tend to be tougher and require more careful preparation and skinning.

CRAB, MUD

Scientific name: Scylla serrata.
Also known as Mangrove crab, muddie, brown mud crab, black mud crab.

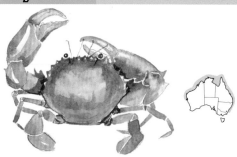

Description: A heavy bodied and heavy clawed crab species which is commonly found near mud banks or flats and mangroves. The body is olive, brown or black and the gripping pegs on the inside of the claws are frequently orange or beige. A very similar species, the green mud crab is found in cleaner water in Western Australia. It is very difficult to differentiate from the more common mud crab other than it is smaller in size, is olive or olive-green in colour and is found in cleaner 'green' water whereas the brown mud crab is found in nearshore tidal and 'brown' water. Mud crabs are much more common in Queensland and the Northern Territory where mangroves and fertile mud flats are more common.

Fishing: Mud crabs can be found in burrows at low tide, frequently in mud banks near mangroves. They move out over the flats as the tide rises. Mud crabs can be caught with a blunt hook in their burrows in some places. This can be a dirty and challenging method as a large and unhappy mud crab looks for something to latch onto upon being removed from its burrow. Mud crabs can severely damage or destroy a witches hat net or hoop drop net. In some areas they are taken in traps, but regulations vary and should be checked. Female mud crabs are protected in Queensland, but the reason is historical much more than biological for this regulation. On capture, the claws of a mud crab are generally tied with twine which involves skill, bravado and dexterity with bare toes and large mud crabs. The mud crab is considered excellent eating which is reflected in the high price to purchase this species. Chili mud crab is one of Queensland's delicacies.

CRAB, SAND

Scientific name: Portunus ovalipes.
Also known as Red-spot crab, surf crab, nicky crab.

Description: A medium sized crab, often found in shallow waters of surf beaches and estuaries. The body is cream or light brown coloured with two distinctive red or maroon spots near the rear of the carapace. A similar species is found from deeper water in Queensland, known as the red-spot crab which has three red spots surrounded by a white fringe.

Fishing: The sand crab is commonly brought to the surge zone in the surf after having grabbed hold of a meat, fish or even squid bait and trying to eat it. The sand crab will often burrow into the sand. The sand crab can be a by-catch when using drop nets for blue swimmer crabs in places such as Geographe Bay in Western Australia, but they are rarely targeted. They are sometimes found in fish shops as commercial beach seiners can take them in reasonable quantities at times. The sand crab is considered quite good eating, but is often small enough to make getting the meat a reasonable task.

CRAB, SOLDIER

Scientific name: Myctiris longicarpus.
Also known as blue army crab.

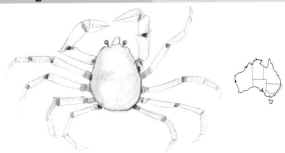

Description: A small and attractive crab of about 25 - 30 mm that emerges in huge numbers from estuarine sand flats, especially those near mangroves. This crab is small with a beautiful sky blue shell. The legs are cream with maroon or light brown leg joints. The soldier crab is very round in shape and the claws are relatively small.

Fishing: At low tide, soldier crabs can be easily gathered by following the legions of crabs that scurry across the flats. Even when approached, they burrow shallowly into the sand and can be dug out easily. They are often taken in small numbers when pumping for nippers. Soldier crabs are used for bream bait and for whiting in estuaries but are less effective than nippers which are often found in similar areas. The soldier crab is an important part of the estuarine ecology and makes a low tide visit to the flats memorable. They can easily be over-exploited so only small numbers should be taken or local requirements followed.

CRAB, BLUE SWIMMER

Scientific name: Portunus pelagicus.
Also known as Blue manna crab, blue swimmer, blue crab, sand crab, bluey.

Description: The blue swimmer crab is an extremely attractive lightly bodied crab with finely textured and very sweet meat. The claws are long and tinged in blue, white or purple. There are no obvious spots on the back of the carapace. They are most commonly found in lower reaches of estuaries. There are obvious points or spikes at the widest point of the body. Queensland and Western Australia measure the blue swimmer crab across the carapace while in NSW the length of the body from between the eyes to the back of the body is used. The belly is white. Males have a narrow pointed flap at the back of the carapace, while in females the flap is broader and may have eggs attached.

Fishing: Blue swimmer crabs are caught with witches hat nets or two hoop drop nets baited with fish or meat. Care should be used when using spleen as bait as it takes a very long time to break down in the water. Witches hat nets are illegal in some states and there are mesh size restrictions so check with the relevant authorities before fishing. In Western Australia blue swimmer crabs can be taken by divers with a scoop net, but taking anything with scuba is prohibited in most parts of Australia. Blue swimmer crabs are sometimes taken on baited lines, although they will usually release the bait near the surface, but a scoop net can catch these tasty crustaceans. Blue swimmer crabs are excellent eating and rated by many as their favourite crustacean.

LIMPET

Scientific name: Family Littorinidae.
Also known as cling shells.

Description: Limpets are small, slightly conical shaped shells which are found on rocky intertidal substrates. They have ridges and are commonly found at the highest level and so are visible (and available) at high tide. The limpet can clam down extremely tightly to the rocks when disturbed and is almost impossible to dislodge. There are similar false limpets which can be picked off the rocks by hand and which appear to rely on camouflage to reduce predation. Interestingly, limpets can return to their exact position on a rock after a feeding forage, apparently following chemical clues in their mucous secretions to their home 'scar' on the rock.

Fishing: Limpets are viewed as the bait of last resort. On the positive side they are tough and withstand pickers but they are not highly prized and can often soak for long periods with little action. There are times when limpets make reasonable bait for bream and trevally but there are generally better baits available.

MUSSEL, BLUE

Scientific name: Mytilus edulis.
Also known as Sea mussel, mussel.

Description: A relatively small mussel species which grows to about 12 cm. The shell is purplish black and the inside of the shell is bluish white. They are wedge shaped and can have a small 'beard' which helps them to attach to substrates such as bridges, jetties and rocks to a depth of up to 10 metres. The blue mussel likes areas of high water movement but needs more than 15 parts per thousand (about half normal sea water to survive)

Fishing: The blue mussel is harvested by hand from areas where they are common and used as bait for bream, whiting and other estuary species. The meat is fairly small and any picker present will remove the bait. Others crush up mussels and use the shells and bits of meat as an excellent burley, but care should be taken not to be too vigorous as this is the food that attracts many fish to the area in the first place. The blue mussel forms part of an extensive aquaculture industry and good catches of fish can be taken in the vicinity. They are excellent eating, with chili mussels one of Perth's specialty dishes. Blue mussels taken from waters with pollution or heavy boat traffic should not be consumed as they can have a petrol 'taint' or could harbour harmful bacteria. They are quite cheap to buy anyway.

OCTOPUS, GLOOMY

Scientific name: Octopus tetricus.
Also known as Occy, inshore octopus.

Description: The gloomy octopus is one of the larger species reaching 80 cm total length and a weight of 3 kilograms. The gloomy octopus differs from other octopus in having long arms which differ in length. The southern octopus reaches a smaller size and has arms of similar length. The octopus is very intelligent but is a much maligned animal, despised by rock lobster fishers and simply viewed as icky by many. The small, blueringed octopus (Hapalochlaena spp.) looks benign at rest with the usual brown camouflage but it can be readily identified by the small electric blue rings which become very bright when disturbed. The beak is right under the animal and only a true idiot or very young child would find themselves with a bitable piece of themselves near the mouth of an angry blue-ringed octopus. However the bite is extremely poisonous. Octopus live for two years and die after mating. The females are much larger and the gloomy octopus can produce around 150,000 eggs which are laid over several nights before passing away and turning into snapper bait.

PRAWN, EASTERN KING

Scientific name: Penaeus plebejus. Also known as king prawn, giant prawn.

Description: A large species which can reach 30 cm in length. The body is flesh coloured, the legs can be reddish in colour and the tail fan can be blue tinged or bright blue in colour. The similar Western king prawn (Penaeus latisculatus) ranges from north Queensland to south of Perth in Western Australia has blue legs.

Fishing: Most Eastern king prawns are taken in commercial nets in deep waters. Juveniles are taken from Moreton Bay in southern Queensland and other southern estuaries and may be scooped or drag netted from these areas when moving to the offshore grounds on the dark of the moon. Some western king prawns are taken at night by scuba divers in the Swan River, where the large size and dexterity needed makes an unusual challenge. All king prawn species are excellent eating and expensive to purchase and as a result are rarely used for bait.

PRAWN, RIVER

Scientific name: Metapenaeus macleayi. Also known as bait prawn, white river prawn.

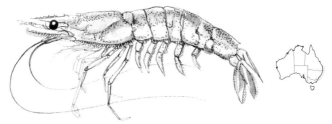

Description: The shell is relatively smooth, the shell lightly sprinkled with very small brown dots on a translucent background. The spike on the tail has four large lateral spines and the head spike or rostrum curves upwards for the end half. The river prawn grows to about 17 cm but is commonly seen at around 10 cm.

Fishing: The river prawn forms the basis of significant recreational and commercial fisheries. During the summer darks of the moon, river prawns make their way from estuaries to oceanic waters to breed. They are taken in scoop nets with a lantern either wading the shallows or from a boat positioned near the channel edge. River prawns are also taken in small drag nets run near the weed beds or sandy flats. They can be taken at all times other than the full moon. Luminescent plankton can make drag netting almost impossible, but it is an enjoyable way to spend an evening and get a feed of tasty prawns. While river prawns are excellent eating, they are also excellent live baits for bream, bass, trevally and mulloway.

PRAWN, SCHOOL

Scientific name: Metapenaeus spp. Also known as bait prawn, schoolie, western school prawn, york prawn, bay prawn, endeavour prawn, greasyback prawn, greentail prawn.

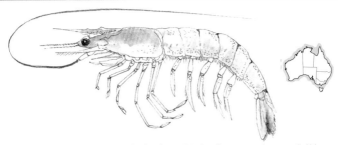

Description: The term school prawn is used to describe a variety of smaller prawn species, many of which are packaged and sold as bait for recreational fishing. The true school prawn, can reach 17 cm and makes a quality meal, but they are harvested by small prawn trawlers in Queensland, NSW and Victoria. The shell is smooth and the rostrum, or head spike is upward pointing which makes it more of a weapon when you are foraging in a bait bag for your next offering. The body has a number of small spots but few anglers would inspect their bait to this degree.

ROCK LOBSTER, EASTERN

Scientific name: Jasus verreauxi. Also known as Eastern crayfish, spiny lobster

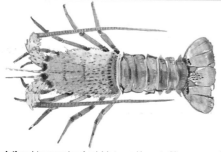

Description: A large species of rock lobster reaching up to 26 cm carapace length and a weight of 8 kilograms. It can live up to 20 years and is found in nearshore waters to deeper reefs. The eastern rock lobster has a green body with orange, orange-brown or brick red legs and most of the tail fan. The main body segments are smooth and importantly the eastern rock lobster lacks horns at the front of the head. The eastern rock lobster is found near the intertidal zone, often need weed and rocky caves where it shelters. They move offshore in winter. In the 1950's, large quantities of eastern rock lobsters were caught by trawling which impacted on the stocks to an extent that is only just now recovering. The tight restrictions on commercial operations has improved the productivity and profitability of the commercial fishery in NSW.

ROCK LOBSTER, ORNATE

Scientific name: Panulirus ornatus.

Also known as Tropical rock lobster, ornate cray, painted cray, painted rock lobster.

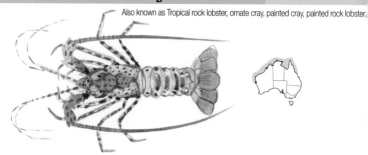

Description: A striking and brightly coloured tropical species which can reach 15cm carapace length. There are several tropical rock lobster species which can appear similar and are often generally referred to as painted crays. The true painted rock lobster (Panulirus versicolor) can appear very similar but tends to be less brightly coloured, with muted greens and green-reds (leading to its Western Australian common name of green rock lobster). The painted rock lobster has distinct long stripes on the legs whereas in the ornate rock lobster the legs have distinct rings and blotches. The back (carapace) of the ornate rock lobster can be bright blue, blue-green or have reddish overtones. The ornate rock lobster forms the basis of a significant commercial fishery in north Queensland and the Torres Straits.

ROCK LOBSTER, SOUTHERN

Scientific name: Jasus edwardsii. Also known as southern crayfish.

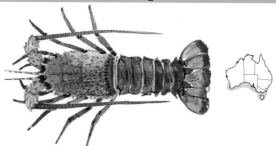

Description: A large and striking rock lobster species which has a rough tail shell and two prominent horns beside the eyes but they do not project past the front of the head. The southern rock lobster can reach 23 cm carapace length. The colour of the southern rock lobster is uniform and is often a shade of dark red.

ROCK LOBSTER, WESTERN

Scientific name: Panulirus cygnus.

Also known as Western crayfish, cray and depending on stage of moult 'white' or 'red' rock lobster.

Description: The Western rock lobster forms the most valuable single species commercial fishery in Australia, with an average harvest of approximately 10.5 million kilograms able to be sustainably harvested each year, with a further 500,000 kilograms of recreationally caught rock lobsters. The Western rock lobster has a rough tail section and the two prominent horns extend past the eyes and the front of the head. They can reach a carapace size of around 16 cm but the fishery more commonly targets a carapace size between 76 and 85 mm. Each year between November and January large numbers of pale orange or light red coloured, recently-moulted juveniles (known as 'whites') migrate from inshore reefs to the deeper reefs offshore. This migration, called the 'whites' run, is the time of most intensive recreational fishing. The recreational fishery is concentrated inside 20 metres deep. Later in the season, adult and non-migrating lobsters are known as 'reds' and form the catch between February and 30 June.

SEA URCHIN, PURPLE

Scientific name: Heliocidaris erythrogramma. Also known as Sea eggs, kina.

Description: Sea urchins are closely related to starfish and sea cucumbers. They move about with tube feet, have a hard external shell usually covered with spines of some description and have the mouth on the underside. The purple sea urchin is important as it forms the basis of a small commercial fishery and is most highly prized by recreational fishers. This species has many spines, with primary spines between 10 and 25 mm long with sharp points while the secondary spines have more blunt tips. The spine colour is generally a deep reddish purple or purple/black with the main shell often a more dirty brown. The purple sea urchin is found in depth of up to 15 metres and in exposed areas concentrates in crevasses where their spines penetrate even the most cautious rock hopper at some time! The purple sea urchin is more common where abalone or rock lobster numbers are low are they are predated upon by these animals.

WORM, BLOOD

Scientific name: Marphysa sanguinea. Also known as Mud worm, wriggler worm, bristle worm.

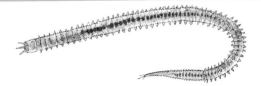

Description: A dark red or brownish red worm that makes its home in the mud, muddy sand or weed of intertidal areas around Australia. They can also be found under rocks in the same areas. The blood worm has a marked purple sheen when it is rinsed after capture and if broken, exudes a considerable amount of 'blood', hence the common name. The blood worm has been recorded at about a 90 cm in length but is most commonly seen at 15 to 20 cm. The blood worm has a pair of sharp jaws which can give a painful bite and they will attack other worms harvested at the same time.

WORM, BEACH

Scientific name: Australonuphis teres.
Also known as Giant beach worm, kingworm, stumpy.

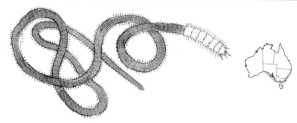

Description: There are a variety of beach worm species that go by the colourful names of slimy, pinky, stripey, wiry, white-head wiry and green. They are all part of the genus Australonuphis sp. (giant and slimy) and Onuphis sp. (others). The beach worms live in the intertidal zone of medium energy beaches. They are extremely strong burrowers and come to the surface to feed on meat or weed. They grab the offering with their head tentacles and arch themselves to tear off a small piece to consume. The giant beach worm can reach nearly 180 cm in length and has a distinctive white head. The common names help to distinguish the other species and finding a good beach wormer in operation will provide many clues about their habits and what is locally prolific.

WORM, SQUIRT

Scientific name: Australonereis ehlersi.
Also known as Sand worm, pump worm, rag worm.

Description: A relatively small worm reaching about 6 cm in length. The squirt worm is found on intertidal sand or sandy mud flats in estuaries in similar habitats to nippers and soldier crabs. They can be located by finding the fine paper-like 'tube' that is actually sand gummed up from mucous as the worms eat. This tube can extend a centimeter or so from the bottom. The squirt worm lives in a tube which has both a front and back entrance. The worm itself is fairly thin and can break apart fairly easily. They do have a reasonable set of jaws but this is rarely enough to bite the fingers. Squirt worms are sand or red coloured.

COCKLE

Scientific name: Katelysia spp. and Anadara spp. Also known as blood cockle.

Description: Differs from the pipi by having a heavier shell with obvious ridges that run down the shell. The cockles prefer less energy areas and are found in sand or sand/mud banks at the backs of estuaries. They can be gathered with the pipi twist but are more commonly dug from recognised cockle beds with a fork or gathered at the absolute bottom of the tide when they may be around.

Fishing: Cockles make an excellent bait for bream, whiting, Australian salmon and other species. They must be shelled and the shells make an excellent berley. The cockle should be hooked through the muscular foot to stay on the hook better. Some anglers use bait elastic to help keep the bait on if there are pickers around. Cockles are also excellent eating if cleaned of sand and lightly steamed.

CRAB, BLACK ROCK

Scientific name: Leptograpsus variegatus Also known as swift-footed rock crab, steelback crab.

Description: The most commonly seen rock crab of temperate Australia but one that can be difficult to catch. The black rock crab varies from a uniform dark olive-green to purple to almost completely black. It is found generally just below or just above the tide line and will scurry away when threatened. They can grow to around 10 cm across the carapace.

Fishing: The black rock crab is seen as a poor substitute to the red rock crab. It can be difficult to catch and does not have the same appeal to groper, bream, snapper and other crab loving species.

CRAB, RED ROCK

Scientific name: Plagusia chabrus. Also known as bait crab, red crab.

Description: The crab is red to brick red and may have white tips to the claws. There is a dense covering of hair on the body and legs. The red rock crab can reach 12 cm across the carapace. The red rock crab is found near the bottom of the intertidal zone where it forages near seaweed and shelters at the base of weed, among the cunjevoi or in rock crevasses.

Fishing: The red rock crab is gathered at low tide when there is a very low swell by walking along the lower tidal area and peeling at the base of seaweed fronds or along crevasses. Some care must be taken as the same crevasses can harbour the dangerous blue-ringed octopus. Although these crabs can be difficult to gather, they are easily the best bait for groper and big bream will be tempted on a half of crab when nothing else works. The crabs should be hooked through the leg socket after the leg is removed and used as berley. Depending on the size of the crab it is fished whole, as a half or in quarters.

CUNJEVOI

Scientific name: Pyura stolonifera. Also known as sea squirt, conjevoi, conjeboy, cunjeboi, cunje.

Description: This is the animal that surprises people when walking on rocks at low tide and getting squirted by water up their legs or onto their face. The cunjevoi is an unusual animal, being born as a larvae with a notochord or primitive backbone, before becoming attached to the rocks and growing its brown leathery coat. Cunjevoi grow in colonies and form their own ecosystem around them, from the absolute bottom of the lowest tide to above the half mean tide on exposed rocks. The cunjevoi feeds through two siphons in the upper surface that appear as a raised, cross shaped 'mouth'. One opening is the entrance for food, the other expels water that has been filtered. The animal which lives inside the tough fibrous skin or test inside of the cunjevoi is a rich brick red or purplish colour and the gonads can be bright orange.

FLYING FISH

Scientific name: Cheilopogon pinnatibarbatus. (Great flying fish, tailfin flying fish, large flying fish) Hirundichthys rondeletii (Rondelet's flying fish, blackwing flying fish) and others.

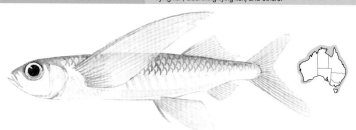

Description: The extremely large and over-developed pectoral fins mean that these fish are easily identified. The ventral fins are also enlarged and aid in stabilising the flying fish while gliding to escape predators. They range from a maximum size of 23 cm for Rondelet's flying fish to 43 cm for the great flying fish.

Fishing: Flying fish feed on plankton and are only taken by recreational anglers when they accidentally fly into a boat. They are however, excellent whole bait for other pelagic predators. Their beautiful gliding is one of the highlights of boat trips when flying fish are common.

GOBY

Scientific name: CFamily Gobiidae. Many common names for various species.

Description: Mainly small species, including one which reaches maturity at 12 mm. Gobies have no lateral line, two clearly separate dorsal fins and the pelvic fins are joined to form a sucker disc. This group includes the mud skippers of tropical areas which can be found clinging to mangroves or hopping over mud at low tide.

Fishing: These are generally forage species which are rarely targeted but several species can make reasonable bait.

HARDYHEAD

Scientific name: Family Atherinidae. Also known as Whitebait.

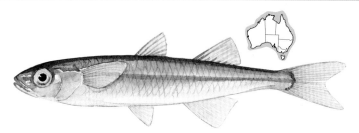

Description: The hardyheads are small forage species reaching a maximum size of 17 cm, but commonly found from 5 to 12 centimetres. They have large tough scales for their size, two separate dorsal fins and a bony head. Marine species are light coloured with a prominent silver stripe along the side. The pectoral fin is placed very high on the body.

Fishing: These are generally marketed as whitebait or hardyheads and are excellent bait for all fish eating species. They are a bit tougher on the hook than bluebait and pilchards. Hardyheads can be caught with fine mesh dip nets or cast nets (where legal) in many estuaries where they form vast schools and can be berleyed with pollard or bread.

MUD SKIPPER

Scientific name: Periopthalmus argentiventralis.
Also known as mud hopper

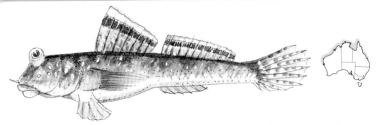

Description: A very unusual species which is often seen at low tide among the exposed mangroves foraging for small crabs, shrimps or stranded fish well above the high tide mark. The mud skipper has an expanded gill chamber which it can fill with water to survive while it 'walks' on its enlarged pectoral fins across the mud flats. When disturbed, the mud skipper uses its tail to move or skip quickly across the flats. The mud skipper can get to 27 cm but many are seen at 8 – 15 centimetres. Their eyes protrude obviously above the head and the first dorsal fin is high and sail like. The mud skipper is well camouflaged for its mangrove mud flats environment and is brown to chocolate. The dorsal fin has a single prominent black stripe and the outer margins may be tinged with red.

Fishing: The mud skipper is very rarely taken by line fishing due to its size. They are often taken in throw nets when fishing for mullet and can be used as live bait. They are good at finding cover and snagging the angler and there are better live baits. This species is a joy to watch in its natural environment and is a curiosity and a special part of tropical mangrove creeks.

NIPPER

Scientific name: Callianassa australiensis. Also known as Bass yabbie, ghost nipper, yabbie, burrowing shrimp, lobby, pink yabby, pink nipper.

Description: A fairly small delicate looking crustacean that lives in holes around 60 cm deep on the sandflats of estuaries. The male nipper has a much enlarged claw which can give quite a painful nip and when removed from the nipper, the muscles contract which makes the claw more difficult to remove. The female has a less well developed large claw and may carry up to 2000 eggs in a cluster under the abdomen. The nipper is generally white or cream and may appear translucent. The eggs may give the abdomen a bright orange appearance before they are laid. The nipper can grow to around 6 cm but are more commonly seen at around 3 centimetres.

PILCHARD

Scientific name: Sardinops sagax neopilchardus. Also known as Sardine, mulie, blue pilchard, Australian pilchard, blue bait, bloater (NZ).

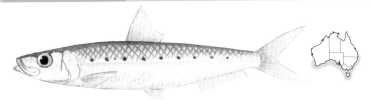

Description: The pilchard is a common schooling forage species of cooler waters taken in large numbers for fishing bait, pet food, aquaculture food and increasingly as a food fish. The pilchard feeds on plankton, using its fairly large mouth and dense gill rakers to filter food. While the pilchard can reach 23 cm, it is commonly used as bait at between 12 and 20 centimetres. The pilchard is very well known to nearly every angler in Australia as the best stand-by bait available. The pilchard has a line of small black spots along the middle part of the body, where the deep blue back changes to the silver belly. The smaller blue sprat (Spratelloides robustus) which is sold as blue sardine or bluebait has a smaller mouth, lacks the black spots on the sides and only reaches 10 centimetres.

PIPI

Scientific name: Plebidonax deltoides.
Also known as ugarie, cockle, goolwa. cockle, Coorang cockle, clam.

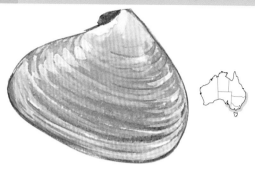

Description: A fairly large bivalve mollusc growing to 7.5 cm across the shell. They have a triangular shell without the obvious circular ridges of the true cockle. The pipi is found in the intertidal area of oceanic beaches where they can be gathered in fairly large numbers on a dropping tide.

Fishing: The pipi can be gathered with a fork in the sand in the wash zone at the bottom of the tide. However, the most common method is to use the pipi twist. Stand in the wash zone and twist both feet together to wriggle into the sand. Pipis will be felt with the toes and can be flicked up when the water won't wash them too far down the beach. Pipis will be no deeper than say ankle deep and a roving approach works well. When pipis are found they are generally in the same depth band along the beach. Some people claim to be able to feel an indent in the sand where a pipi is found, but I have never found this. Pipis can also be gathered by hand at the very bottom of neap tides when they seem to wash to the bottom of the tidal zone. Care should be taken not to over harvest pipis as excessive catches and black marketing them for bait has led to bag limits in NSW. Pipis are an excellent bait for all surf species from whiting to school mulloway. Australian salmon have a special fondness for pipi. The hook should be placed in the foot so that it stays on the hook. Pipis are actually much under-rated for their eating qualities, but they should be purged or rinsed as they can contain a fair bit of sand which adds an unwelcome crunch to the pipi dish.

RAZORFISH

Scientific name: Solen correctus Also known as Chinaman's fingernail.

Description: An unusual bivalve mollusc, whose narrow shell is known as the Chinaman's fingernail. The razorfish lives on sheltered ocean beaches or in estuaries usually only a few centimetres below the surface but when disturbed, can burrow through the sand much more quickly than a man can dig. The razor fish burrows with its prominent muscular foot which is yellow and is larger than the shells. The razorfish is sometimes confused with the razor clam (Pinna menkei) which is a large triangular shelled mollusc that grows in sandy or muddy estuaries and mangrove areas and which can cut the feet of the unwary wader.

Fishing: The razorfish is an excellent bait for King George whiting and other whiting species. It is gathered either by digging with a spade which is hard work as disturbed razorfish will dive out of range, or by using a wire hook forced down the burrows and then dragging the animal out. The razorfish is extremely common in the Gulf of St Vincent and Spencer Gulf and along the Eyre Peninsula in South Australia.

SAURIE

Scientific name: Scomberesox saurus. Also known as King gar, Saury, Billfish, Skipper.

Description: The saurie is a garfish relative easily distinguished by two short, slender but toothless jaws and 6 to 7 finlets behind both the dorsal and anal fins. This species is frequently found in offshore waters, skipping across the wake of passing boats. Saury schools can enter large coastal bays during summer.

Fishing: The saurie is an excellent trolling bait for large pelagic species although it is rarely available, except through fish shops at certain times. This is not a target recreational angling species.

SARDINE

Scientific name: Amblygaster leiogaster.
Also known as Blue sardine, blue sprat, bluebait.

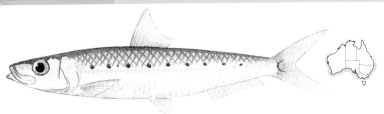

Description: The sardine is a small schooling species reaching only 10 cm which often shelters near shallow reefs in large numbers. Apart from its size, this species is distinguished by it smaller eye and black horseshoe shaped mark near the base of the tail.

Fishing: This is a plankton feeder that is never caught by angling methods. The sardine is one of the most under-rated baits, possessing the oily flesh of the larger pilchard, but in a size better suited to species like bream, Australian herring, small Australian salmon and chopper tailor. Sardines can be threaded on a larger hook, or preferably fished on gangs of No 2 or 1 hooks.

SILVER BIDDY

Scientific name: Gerres subfasciatus. Also known as roach, silverbiddy, common silverbelly, blacktip silverbelly, ovate silverbelly.

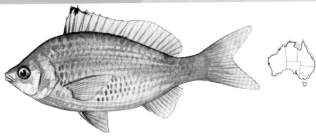

Description: A common forage species found in coastal bays and estuaries throughout its range. The quite small mouth of the silver biddy is in the middle of the small head. The eye is quite large and the fins are translucent. The front of the dorsal fin has a prominent black blotch. The silver biddy differs from the southern silverbelly (Parequula melbournensis) which is found in southern waters and only overlaps in range from Rottnest Island to Albany in Western Australia and lacks the black spot on the dorsal fin. The southern silverbelly is also more rounded in body shape and the eye appears even larger.

Fishing: The silver biddy is most often taken in cast nets in tropical waters where it is highly valued as a live bait for species such as flathead, snapper and mackerel. They can be attracted by berley and taken in throw nets or with bait jigs. The silver biddy is not highly regarded as a food fish.

SPRAT

Scientific name: Spratelloides robustus. Also known as Blue sprat, bluebait, blue sardine.

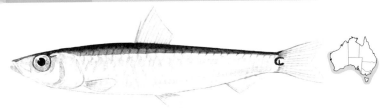

Description: A small schooling species common around inshore reefs, the sprat reaches 10 cm in length. The sprat is most easily identified by a black horseshoe shaped mark at the base of the tail fin abd has no spots. The sprat is bluish green on the back which differentiates it from the sandy, translucent colour of the similar sized whitebait.

Fishing: The sprat is not taken by recreational anglers but is an excellent and frequently under-rated bait for many species. The bluebait can be fished on a single hook or on a gang of small linked hooks in number 1 – 4 in a scaled down version of the ganged hook rig used with pilchards.

WHIPTAIL

Scientific name: Pentapodus paradiseus.
Also known as Paradise whiptail, bluefaced whiptail, paradise-fish, rainbow.

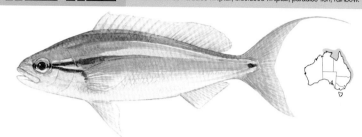

Description: A strikingly beautiful fish, which only reaches around 23 centimetres. The nose is brilliantly striped with blue and gold or yellow horizontal stripes which extend to around the beginning of the eye. There is a long lateral yellow stripe along the midline, with a gold-brown stripe running below. There is also a yellow stripe running from the back of the mouth to the lower edge of the pectoral fin and a bright blue stripe along the base of the dorsal fin. This species gets its name from their elongated upper lobe of the yellow or pink-yellow tail fin. There is also a prominent black spot at the base of the tail fin. This small fish can form quite large schools in large estuaries or near inshore weedy reefs.

Fishing: The whiptail is highly regarded as a baitfish either fished dead or as a cut bait for bottom species such as snapper or fished as a hardy live bait for Spanish mackerel, tuna and other tropical pelagics. Once a school is located, they can be caught on lightly weighted rigs with small hooks baited with worms, prawns, squid or fresh flesh.

WHITEBAIT

Scientific name: Hyperlophus vittatus.
Also known as Sandy sprat, glassy, white pilchard.

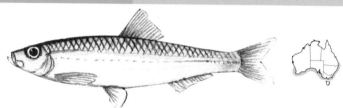

Description: The whitebait is a schooling forage species common in coastal bays, off beaches and in the mouths of estuaries. The whitebait can be separated from the hardyheads which are often marketed as whitebait by the single dorsal fin while hardyheads have two dorsal fins. The whitebait reaches 10 cm in length and is often available at 6 – 9 centimetres.

Fishing: The whitebait is an excellent bait species which stays on the hook better than the softer bluebait. Whitebait is best fished on a gang of smaller number 6 to 1 hooks depending on the size of the baits.

WHITEBAIT, TASMANIAN

Scientific name: Lovettia sealii.

Description: The Tasmanian whitebait is a small species reaching less than 8 cm and commonly seen at around 6 centimetres. It is fished for as it migrates upstream out of estuaries. Another species, the jollytail or common trout minnow (Galaxias maculatus) is also sold as small transparent whitebait but the Tasmanian whitebait has a more restricted range, an adipose fin and a more concave tail.

Fishing A common and important forage species, the adults of which are favourites as bait for sea run trout. Juveniles are fished in special nets. Tasmanian whitebait can occasionally be found in Victoria where they are totally protected.

AUSTRALIA'S TOP KNOTS

Arbor Knot

This is a very fast and secure knot for attaching line to the reel. Pass the tag end of the line around the spool and form an overhand knot with the tag end around around the main line. Then another overhand knot on the tag end of the line. Lubricate the knots if using monofilament, tighten down by pulling the main line, and trim the tag.

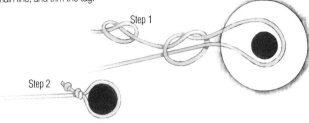

Clinch Knot

Thread the line through the hook eye and wrap the end back up the line five times. Thread the leader back through the first loop in front of the hook eye. Lubricate the knot and pull steadily to tighten it against the hook eye. When tightening, hold the tag end of the tippet against the hook to avoid knot slippage. Trim the tag end.

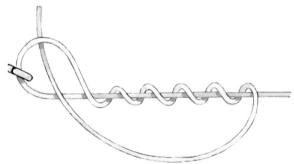

Uni Knot

An easy-to-tie versatile knot. Thread the eye of the hook with the line so the hook is suspended on a loop. Encircle the main line with the tag so another loop is formed. Wrap the double strand inside the loop with the tag. Make four wraps in all, leaving the tag protruding from the loop. Close the knot but do not pull it tight just yet. Slide the knot down onto the eye of the hook, pull it tight and trim the tag.

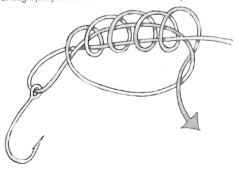

AUSTRALIA'S TOP KNOTS

Trilene Knot

A strong kno for tying medium hooks to 6–15 kg line. Thread the line through the hook eye twice and wrap it back up the line five times. Thread the line back through the two loops formed at the hook eye. Lubricate the knot and pull steadily to tighten the knot against the eye of the hook. When tightening, hold the tag end of the line against the hook to avoid knot slippage. Trim the tag end of the line.

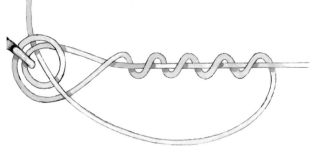

Blood Knot

This is the most frequently used knot for joining two sections of like-diameter monofilament. Cross two 5 cm (4 inch) lengths of linel over each other and hold the cross formed with your right thumb and forefinger. Use your left hand to make five turns with the short end of the line around the long section, twisting away from your thumb and forefinger. Bring back the short end and insert it through the other side of the crossed lines. Now switch the knot over from your right to left thumb and forefinger, and repeat the

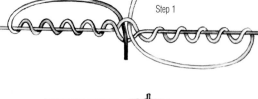

Step 1

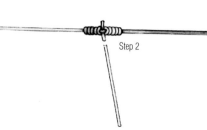

Step 2

process using the left tag end. Bring the tag back as before and thread it through the centre loop formed, but in the opposite direction to right hand tag. Lubricate the loose knot with saliva and draw the knot tight before trimming the tag ends close to the knot. This knot makes an excellent dropper knot. When you start to tie this knot, simply allow one of the tag ends to be about 15–30 cm (6–12 inches) long. At the completion of the knot, trim the short tag end only, leaving the longer tag for the dropper.

AUSTRALIA'S TOP KNOTS

Homer Rhode Knot

This knot should never be used on lighter weight monofilaments, as it breaks at around 50 per cent of the line test.

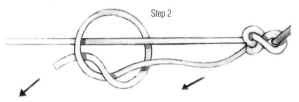

Step 1

Form an overhand knot in the main line leaving approximately 20 cm (8 inches) of monofilament between the knot and the tag end. Pass the tag end through the hook eye and then back through the overhand knot from the same side as it exited. Tighten the overhand knot lightly to the hook eye by pulling on the tail of the hook and on the tag end of the line, while keeping the two lines parallel to prevent the hook from twisting on the knot.

Step 2

Make another overhand knot over thestanding part of the line. This knot is the stopper for the loop, so its position determines the size of the loop, generally this knot would be 2–3 cm (1 inch) from the hook eye. Tighten this second knot and then pull on the bend of the hook and the main line at the same time.

Step 3

The knot at the hook eye should slide up the line snugly into the second knot. Trim the tag.

Double Surgeon's Knot

The quickest knot for joining two sections of leader and is especially useful when the sections are very different in diameter. Overlap two sections of line by about 15 cm (6 inches). Form a 5 cm (2 inch) loop and tie in three overhand knots through the large loop. Lubricate the knot and pull steadily on all four ends to tighten. Trim the tag ends closely to the formed knot. This knot is often used to form a
dropper, but is best used only when speed is of the essence as both the Double Grinner Knot and the Blood Knot make better droppers by allowing the droppers to stand at right angles to the main line.

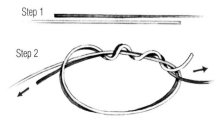

Step 1

Step 2

AUSTRALIA'S TOP KNOTS

Albright Knot

The Albright Knot is a standard knot and is used when joining lines that are very different in diameter or when joining wire to monofilament.

Form a loop in the tag end of the heavier line or wire making sure you allow 15 cm (6 inches) to overlap. Take the lighter line and pass the tag through the formed loop. Pinch both lines about 8 cm (3 inches) from the end, and at the same time allow approximately 8 cm (3 inches) of the lighter line to protrude beyond this point to tie the knot. Start winding the lighter line back towards the end loop. Make at least ten tight turns of the lighter material back over the doubled section. Pass the lighter material through the end loop on the same side of the loop that the lighter line originally entered. Very slowly, pull on the lighter line ends while grasping the heavier section and working the coils of the knot towards the loop end. Do not allow the coils to slip off the loop. Take special care when tying this knot as is very prone to slipping if it is not tightened correctly.

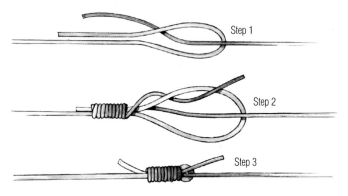

Loop to Loop

When using loop to loop connections for your leader to the main line, it is critical that the two loops sit correctly. This illustration shows the correct method. If these loops are not correctly joined then it is possible for the lines to cut into each other and destroy the integrity of the knot.

Connect the lines by sliding one loop over the other loop. Thread the leader loop through the main line loop and pull the connections tight so that the loops join.

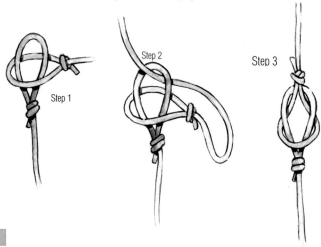

AUSTRALIA'S TOP KNOTS

Spider Hitch

This is an easy to tie and effective double line loop which is good for attaching small diameter lines to large diameter lines. Although quick to tie, it is not as effective as the Bimini Twist Knot.

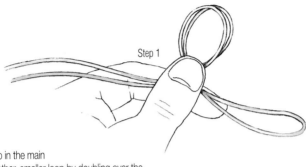

Step 1

Form a large loop in the main line and form another, smaller loop by doubling over the already doubled lines between thumb and forefinger.

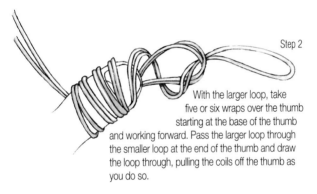

Step 2

With the larger loop, take five or six wraps over the thumb starting at the base of the thumb and working forward. Pass the larger loop through the smaller loop at the end of the thumb and draw the loop through, pulling the coils off the thumb as you do so.

Lubricate the loose knot and tighten it by pulling on the main line and tag and the loop at the opposite end. Trim the tag.

Step 3

TOP SALTWATER RIGS

Sabiki Bait Jigs

If it's important that you need to catch a number of live baits in a hurry, the multi-hook bait jig is super-effective. They catch a heap of slimy mackerel, yackas and similar livies. Ensure that this style of bait rig isn't against local Fisheries regulations, as it could land you a fine in some states!

Start a light berley trail to attract the baitfish, then drop the lot over the side amongst them and wait for them to climb on. There's no bait needed as the glitter and flash built into the rig does the job for you. Sometimes you can locate bait schools with the help of an echo sounder and simply drop the jig rig down into them.

Sabiki style bait rigs come with various sizes and various numbers of hooks, but again, ensure you use those permitted in your state. Attach a sinker to the bottom of the rig (choose weight according to the tide and water depth) and move the rig up and down slowly to attract the baitfishes' attention.

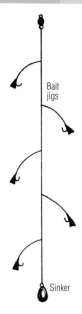

Bait jigs

Sinker

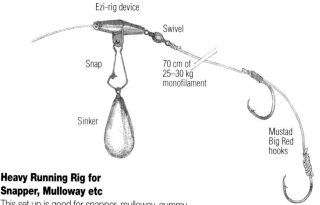

Ezi-rig device

Swivel

Snap

70 cm of 25–30 kg monofilament

Sinker

Mustad Big Red hooks

Heavy Running Rig for Snapper, Mulloway etc

This set up is good for snapper, mulloway, gummy sharks and many other inshore fish that can be picky about the way they feed. The theory behind a running rig is simple: it provides enough weight to get your bait down to where it's needed, but allows the fish to take off with your bait under minimal resistance.

A favourite running sinker rig for larger fish consists of an Ezi-Rig style clip (available from most tackle stores quite cheaply), a rolling swivel, a 70 cm length of nylon leader and a couple of hooks. The Ezi-Rig clip is a great idea that enables you to change sinker weights quickly. Use the minimum amount of lead you can get away with and carry a range of sinkers to cover most tidal conditions. Use a good quality straight or snap swivel to connect main line and leader, and go for 25–30 kg monofilament trace. This is easily strong enough for snapper, gummy sharks and mulloway. Hook choice will depend on the fish you are chasing, but suicide patterns like the Mustad Big Red are excellent.

TOP SALTWATER RIGS

Swivel

Fixed sinker

South Australian King George Whiting Rig

This whiting rig is straightforward. Tie one hook above and one below a fixed sinker. Hook size varies from #6 for smaller fish to #2 for the big ones. Trace material is monofilament and usually 8–10 kg breaking strain. Long shank hooks like the Mustad Bloodworm are preferred.

Heavy Paternoster Rig for Deep Water

The paternoster rig is universally popular across the country. It's a very simple rig, with two hooks off separate droppers above an appropriate size sinker. The paternoster is usually joined to the mainline via a swivel and can be used for a variety of fish species.

It's appropriate for small to medium snapper, pearl perch, trevally and many other fish in medium to deep water. When tied correctly it doesn't tangle badly and is an easy rig to assemble—a couple of dropper loops to connect each hook trace and a large figure eight loop at the bottom for the sinker. Keep the hook droppers reasonably short to minimise tangles and make sure they are placed well apart. Hook size depends on the fish you're after and sinker weight depends on both tide and water depth.

Dropper loop

Dropper loop

Figure eight loop

Sinker

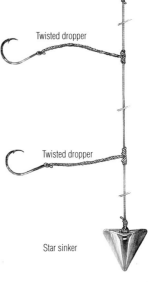

Twisted dropper

Twisted dropper

Star sinker

Twisted Dropper Surf Rig

This is an effective rig for catching Australian salmon from the beach. Tie a couple of extra long dropper loops about 60 cm apart in the trace, then twist the loops to form strong leaders.

Slip two hooks of the right size (usually 3/0 to 5/0) on to the end of each twisted dropper, tie a star sinker to the bottom of the rig and you're ready to bait up. Put a half pilchard (or fish fillets, squid and even prawns) on each hook. Make sure you use a good quality snap or barrel swivel between trace and main line to eliminate twist.

TOP SALTWATER RIGS

Surface Float Rig

An excellent surface salmon rig consists of a styrene float, a couple of 4/0 hooks and a small sinker for weight. The hooks are tied on a metre or so of 15 kg monofilament trace and are spaced to hold a full pilchard comfortably. Slip a running ball sinker down the trace right on to the top hook. Then slip on a running styrene float and attach the top of the trace to a good quality swivel. This will allow the float to suspend your bait at the correct depth for feeding salmon. Should you require the bait to be set deeper, simply extend the trace length.

This rig casts reasonably well from a threadline or sidecast outfit and can be modified easily to suit small or large salmon, tommy ruff, tailor (with the inclusion of a light wire trace) and trevally.

Main line

Swivel

Glitterbug float

Sinkerr

Shallow Water/Non-Tidal Snapper Rig

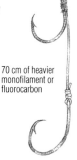

One of the most basic, yet most effective rigs for snapper, bream and other inshore fish has no sinker and can be assembled in seconds. Connect your main line to a good quality swivel and then attach 70 cm of heavier monofilament or fluorocarbon leader. Use leaders of 25 kg for big snapper or 4–6 kg for bream.

You can use single or twin hooks spaced them to suit the type of bait on this rig. The top hook free can be allowed to run free on the trace rather than snelled.

This rig can only be used in areas of minimal tide flow, which restricts its use somewhat.

70 cm of heavier monofilament or fluorocarbon

Ezi-rig device

Swivel

Snap

Sinker

8/0–10/0 Mustad Big Reds or Gamakatsu Octopus

Surf Mulloway Rig

Take twin 8/0–10/0 hooks (usually Mustad Big Reds or Gamakatsu Octopus) tied on 60 cm of 80 pound nylon trace and attached to a high quality swivel.

Tie 70–80 cm of 80 pound mono to the top of that swivel and thread on an Ezi-Rig device as a sinker attachment. A second swivel is tied to the top of the rig, which stops the sinker and acts as a joiner between trace and main line. While slightly cumbersome to cast, this rig is effective on the big jewies.

TOP SALTWATER RIGS

Main line

Brass ring

200 – 500 gram barrel sinker

Brass ring

Hard-coated nylon leader

Mustad hoodlum (8/0–11/0)

Deep Water Live Bait Rig

When kingfish are stacked up over a reef in deep water, a struggling live bait is definitely the way to go. The most effective live bait rig consists of a high quality hook like the Mustad Hoodlum (8/0–11/0), a length of hard coated monofilament leader, a heavy barrel or bean sinker and a couple of heavy duty brass rings. Snell or crimp the hook to about a metre of 100 pound leader and attach this to one of the brass rings. A second, short length of leader material is also attached to that ring, slide the sinker on and then tie on the second ring. This second ring can then be tied directly to a double in the main line or to the end of a wind-on leader. It's a tough trace for tough fish.

Ball sinker

Swivel

Light Running Rig for Bream, Flathead etc.

Bream, flathead, sand whiting, mullet and similar estuary or bay species are best tackled with light gear and a rig that produces least resistance. Next to a rig with no sinker at all, a basic running sinker set up is usually best. Thread the sinker (usually a ball, bean or barrel) directly on to the main line and allow it to run down to a small swivel. The swivel acts as a stopper as well as a connector between line and trace. To the opposite end of the swivel, attach 50 cm of monofilament leader and a single hook. Select the leader appropriate to the fish. Use 4–6 kg for bream and sand whiting, and 10 kg for flathead. This rig is best used with a 'Baitrunner' style threadline reel.

50 cm of monofilament

TOP SALTWATER TECHNIQUES

TECHNIQUE 1

Cast soft plastics to the top of the bank and retrieve over the edge. Always ensure the plastic is allowed to sink back to the bottom during pauses in the retrieve.

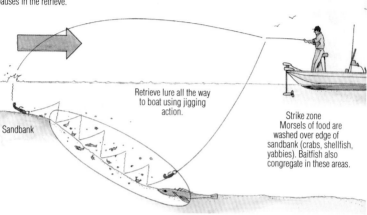

Retrieve lure all the way to boat using jigging action.

Sandbank

Strike zone
Morsels of food are washed over edge of sandbank (crabs, shellfish, yabbies). Baitfish also congregate in these areas.

Serious Flathead

There are some big flathead out there in our tidal estuaries. An area that produces really well for these bruisers is where the current runs over a shallow bank and into deeper water. Flatties lay in ambush along these edges in the deeper water, feeding on crabs, yabbies, worms and even little fish that get pushed down the face of the sand bank by the out-going tide.

To get into the action in these areas, use a decent sized soft plastic on a jighead. Cast it to the top of the bank, then retrieve it over the edge and jig it down the bank, into deeper water and back to the boat. This can be a sure-fire way to crack it for a big flathead at places like Port Albert, Narooma, Stradbroke Island and a whole host of other spots.

TECHNIQUE 2

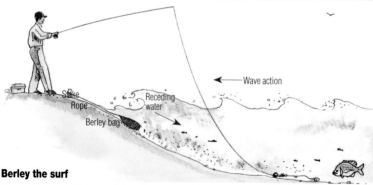

Wave action

Stake
Rope

Receding water

Berley bag

Berley the surf

If you get too sea sick to go offshore, then try surf fishing. Using a full berley bag thrown into the surf lets the wave action do all the work for you. Remember to berley on an incoming tide, otherwise the wave action will keep moving the berley bag and stop attracting fish. A berley bag in the surf works all over Australia on salmon, bream, whiting, tailor and a whole host of species. The serious guys get into some monster mulloway off the surf beaches in the Great Australian Bight!

TOP SALTWATER TECHNIQUES

TECHNIQUE 3

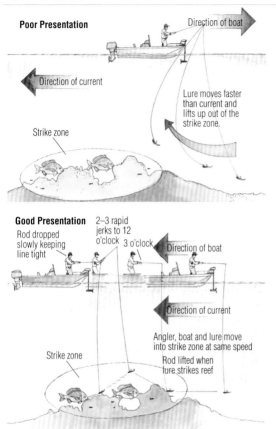

Poor Presentation

Direction of boat

Direction of current

Lure moves faster than current and lifts up out of the strike zone.

Strike zone

Good Presentation

Rod dropped slowly keeping line tight

2–3 rapid jerks to 12 o'clock

3 o'clock

Direction of boat

Direction of current

Angler, boat and lure move into strike zone at same speed

Strike zone

Rod lifted when lure strikes reef

Drifting and fishing soft plastics

When fishing a deeper reef in an estuary, you'll always get a better presentation if you can coincide your fishing with the tide and wind running in the same direction. This way you can work the bow of your boat into the tide and the wind, and hold over the reef. This allows a good deep water presentation of the soft plastic rigged jighead.

Once the jig is down in the strike zone, back off on the electric motor, and drift back over the reef, working the jig down near the reef.

TECHNIQUE 4

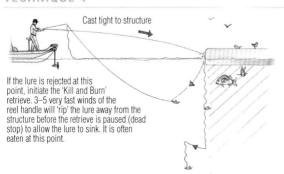

Cast tight to structure

If the lure is rejected at this point, initiate the 'Kill and Burn' retrieve. 3–5 very fast winds of the reel handle will 'rip' the lure away from the structure before the retrieve is paused (dead stop) to allow the lure to sink. It is often eaten at this point.

The Dead Sink

As the name implies, this approach involves allowing the lure to sink as naturally as possible. It sounds simple, but I still see many anglers struggling with this aspect of the technique. Firstly, cast the lure into the desired location. As the

lure lands, keep the bail arm open and using a quick flick of the rod, shake some excess line off the spool. As you get better at it, and when your spool is full of line, the flick will not produce the slightest movement of the soft plastic lure.

TOP SALTWATER TECHNIQUES

TECHNIQUE 5

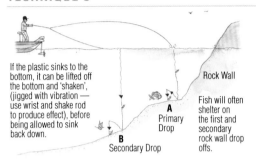

If the plastic sinks to the bottom, it can be lifted off the bottom and 'shaken', (jigged with vibration — use wrist and shake rod to produce effect), before being allowed to sink back down.

Rock Wall

Fish will often shelter on the first and secondary rock wall drop offs.

A Primary Drop

B Secondary Drop

Hop and Shake

This retrieve is adopted where an angler believes fish will be holding near the bottom. The lure is permitted to sink all the way to the bottom, at which point it is lifted gently off the bottom while shaking the rod tip. The rod tip is moved enough to lift the soft plastic 10 to 20 centimetres off the bottom before the lure is allowed to move in "dead sink" style back to the bottom. This is repeated two to three times before the lure is retrieved and cast to the next likely looking spot.

TECHNIQUE 6

Bibless Rattling Minnows

Bibless minnows are a great new option for saltwater. As they sink fast they're ideal for working bottom structure on species like flathead, mulloway and even snapper! You'll be surprised at what you'll catch!

• Keeping the lure in the strike zone for as long as possible. Many anglers fish this technique too quickly. The result is the lure travelling above the strike zone for much of the retrieve. Once you have got your lure into the key area, don't be shy to just leave it there, imparting little lifts and jerks occasionally. The beauty of using these lures is that you are able to keep them in the

Cast your lure past the point where you expect it to reach the target location. This ensures that as the lure sinks back towards you while drifting it ends up in the zone when ypou reach the stage of the drift.

Cast lure across current so it's in line with your position in the current.

Target Location

Keep your line tight as you drift to ensure you a the lure maintain the same line within the current. If the lure falls behind, you will start to drag the lure unnaturally quick

Cast the lure then:
1. Keep the rod tip at 2 O'clock and with the line tight let the lure sink.
2. As the lure hits the bottom, the line will slacken. Drop the rod to 3 o'clock as you retrieve loose line.
3. Give the rod two quick lifts to take the rod to 1 o'clock. Drop the rod to 2 o'clock retrieving slcak line and then repeat steps 1, 2 and 3.

Baitball

The retrieve continues as the boat, angler and lure drift down the current at the same line within the current.

key fish holding areas for longer than other lure prototypes.

• Always try to visualise what the lure is doing down on the bottom. Try to fish the lure right into the structure you have identified as a key fish holding zone. Adapt your technique to keep the lure in this zone as long as possible.

• Always let the lure sink with the line kept tight. This allows you to produce a slower sink rate of the lure. When you get this right, it makes it hard for a nearby fish to leave the presentation alone.

TOP FRESHWATER RIGS

Running Sinker Rigs for Rivers and Lakes

Here is your standard shore based rig in freshwater for anything that swims in rivers and lakes. The running sinker rig is ideal for fishing worms in rivers and lakes for trout, shrimp for bass and redfin and little mullet for barra. Two red beads will add to the attraction, they're my favourite way of adding a bit extra to the situation and just maybe tipping the scales a bit more my way.

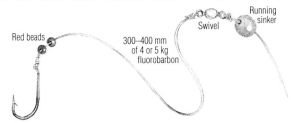

Running sinker

Swivel

Red beads

300–400 mm of 4 or 5 kg fluorobarbon

Bobbing Worms for Active Fishing

This little rig is a beauty and probably not all that well known, and it's a real good one to add to your stable of deliveries. It's like a running sinker rig but the sinker is relocated between the swivel and the hook. The idea is to cast it out and bob or jig it very slowly back in. Don't just leave it sitting on the bottom—work it! Again the beads add attraction and remember just use 3 kilo line, no more. You'll catch lots of fish on this rig fished slowly this way.

Swivel

Beads

Running sinker above coloured beads

300–400 mm of 4 or 5 kg fluorobarbon

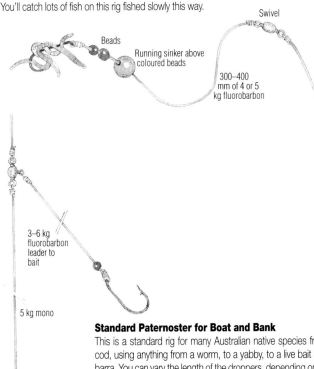

3–6 kg fluorobarbon leader to bait

5 kg mono

Fixed teardrop sinker

Standard Paternoster for Boat and Bank

This is a standard rig for many Australian native species from barra to cod, using anything from a worm, to a yabby, to a live bait or prawn for barra. You can vary the length of the droppers, depending on conditions, and the 3-way swivel could be substituted with a brass ring if the fish encountered are likely to pull your arms off! Add a red bead too—it can add a touch of spark and get those fish biting.

TOP FRESHWATER RIGS

Running Sinker Rigs with Dinner Bells

Yabbies are everywhere in southern Australia's lakes and dams and are one of the best and most popular baits in this part of the country. Normally, the rig to fish a yabby is a simple running rig, but try this one with two sinkers.

It makes a bit more noise and clatter and could help wake up some of those native fish hanging around where you're fishing. It's ideal for rigging around trees and could make all the difference.

Two sinkers rigged between 2 brass rings will send out sonic signals when the rig is bounced.

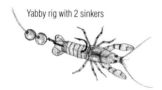

Yabby rig with 2 sinkers

Mudeye bubble float rig

When trout fishing, using mudeyes is a dynamite way to catch them. Mudeyes are an early stage in the dragon fly life cycle. The best way to present a mudeye is under a bubble float. The bubble float can be ½ or ¾ filled with water to assist casting and to supply extra resistance if there is a wind. Use a small piece of sliced cork to act as a stopper. Set the distance between the cork and the mudeye to the depth that you want the mudeye to swim. The cork floats and the mudeye isn't strong enough to pull it under. When you're fishing deep and want the mudeye to go deep too, then use a long rod and hold the extra drop down in your hand prior to casting—refer to the illustration. When hooking the mudeye use a small fly hook, size 12, and hook your mudeye through the wings only—this will ensure it swims freely and does not die before a trout takes it.

Night bait rig

Slingshot casting

Deep water bubble rig

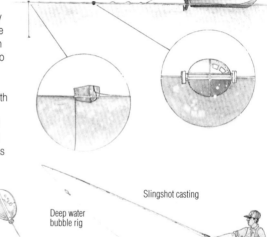

TOP FRESHWATER TECHNIQUES

TECHNIQUE 1

Slow rolling soft plastics along the margins of weedbeds, vertically and tight against submerged timber, or through schools of sounded fish.

Soft plastics will work well on shut down fish but the lure has to be presented right on the nose of fish and must be worked with a slow, consistent retrieve rate. The key to this technique is to cast the soft plastic in tight to the structure where you believe fish will be holding. Allow the plastic to reach the depth where fish are likely to be and then slowly and consistently wind the lure through the strike zone.

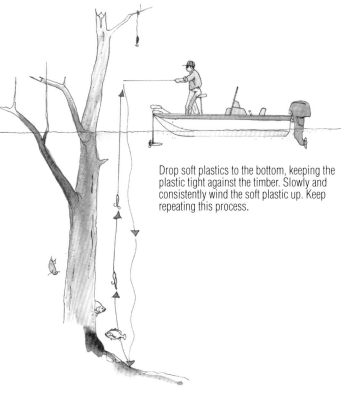

Drop soft plastics to the bottom, keeping the plastic tight against the timber. Slowly and consistently wind the soft plastic up. Keep repeating this process.

TOP FRESHWATER TECHNIQUES

TECHNIQUE 2

Using rattling and silent lipless crankbaits and fishing them either slowly or with fast retrieves through fish holding structures such as drop-offs, weedbeds and timber. Casting these lures close to structure and then by using short rod lifts and pauses with the line kept tight, a lure can be kept in the strike zone for short periods.

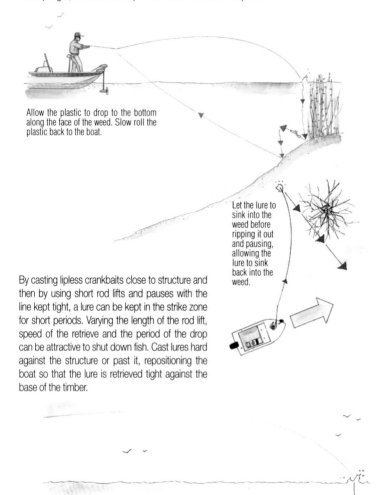

Allow the plastic to drop to the bottom along the face of the weed. Slow roll the plastic back to the boat.

Let the lure to sink into the weed before ripping it out and pausing, allowing the lure to sink back into the weed.

By casting lipless crankbaits close to structure and then by using short rod lifts and pauses with the line kept tight, a lure can be kept in the strike zone for short periods. Varying the length of the rod lift, speed of the retrieve and the period of the drop can be attractive to shut down fish. Cast lures hard against the structure or past it, repositioning the boat so that the lure is retrieved tight against the base of the timber.

TOP FRESHWATER TECHNIQUES

TECHNIQUE 3

Fishing spinnerbaits or suspending hardbodied lures in tight against timber, ensuring the lure is bumped through the structure as much as possible and paused close to the structure.

These types of lure work well when bumped into submerged structure. Spinnerbaits that are fished with a slow, consistent retrieve with slight pauses.

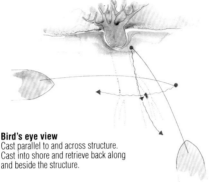

Bird's eye view
Cast parallel to and across structure. Cast into shore and retrieve back along and beside the structure.

Drop the spinnerbait down alongside the timber, then slowly and consistently wind back. Bump the lure through the timber, pausing after passing the timber to drop the lure into the strike zone. Retrieve the lure until it is bumped into timber. Pause and allow it to float over or walk through the structure. Pause as the lure passes the structure to allow it to hang in the strike zone.

TECHNIQUE 4

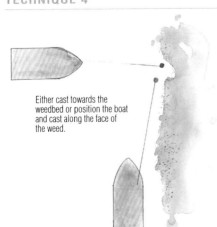

Either cast towards the weedbed or position the boat and cast along the face of the weed.

Target the margins of the waterway because if there is the occasional fish active, this is where they will be found.
Use lipless crank-baits and small hardbodied lures.

TOP FRESHWATER TECHNIQUES

TECHNIQUE 5

For submerged, isolated structures sitting in 3–7 m of water along steep, sloping banks, position your boat within casting range and cast past and roll retrieve back to the boat.

The roll cast is achieved by winding continuously while rolling your wrists, and the rod tip, in a figure-of-eight motion. Alternatively, cast over, helicopter down then flat retrieve back to the boat. It's always best if you can position your boat on the shallow or rising bank side of the snag.

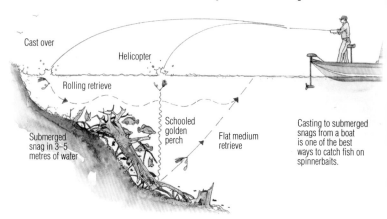

Cast over

Helicopter

Rolling retrieve

Schooled golden perch

Submerged snag in 3–5 metres of water

Flat medium retrieve

Casting to submerged snags from a boat is one of the best ways to catch fish on spinnerbaits.

TECHNIQUE 6

Most impoundments have huge stands of vertical timber—usually hundreds of trees.

Start with the isolated ones, the bigger the better. Any flooded, standing tree sitting in 3–8 m of water is worth putting a cast past and working a rolling retrieve or a helicopter cast beside it.

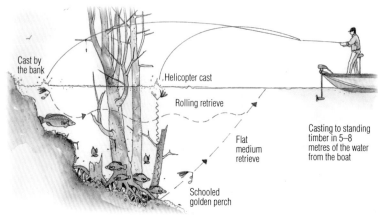

Cast by the bank

Helicopter cast

Rolling retrieve

Flat medium retrieve

Casting to standing timber in 5–8 metres of the water from the boat

Schooled golden perch

TOP FRESHWATER TECHNIQUES

TECHNIQUE 7

Fishing the banks while afloat can be much more productive than just parking and walking. Spinnerbait retrieves in this situation can be as simple as cast and retrieve, cast and drop to the bottom (sometimes a thirty count to be sure) then a retrieve, a roll retrieve from the deep and deep water 'walk the dog'

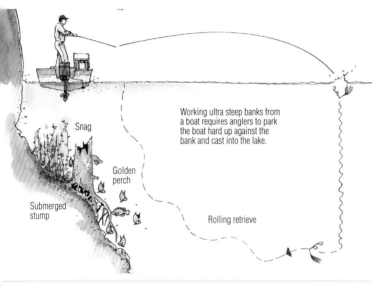

Working ultra steep banks from a boat requires anglers to park the boat hard up against the bank and cast into the lake.

Snag

Golden perch

Submerged stump

Rolling retrieve

TECHNIQUE 8

Casting over weedbeds during late spring will consistently produce fish. Concentrate on working the spinnerbait up the slope behind the weedbed. You'll get your share of hang-ups on weed, but you'll get plenty of fish too.

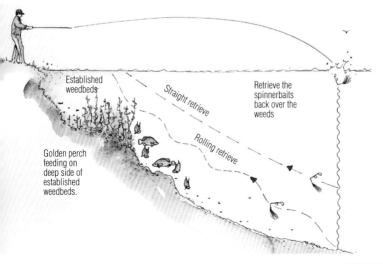

Established weedbeds

Straight retrieve

Retrieve the spinnerbaits back over the weeds

Rolling retrieve

Golden perch feeding on deep side of established weedbeds.

TOP FRESHWATER TECHNIQUES

TECHNIQUE 9

Passive retrieve

The aim of this retrieve is to simulate a juvenile fish searching for food in the sediment on the bottom. **Step 1:** Cast and allow the lure to sink to the bottom. **Step 2:** As soon as the lure has hit the bottom start the retrieve. **Step 3:** Lift the rod from a 2 o'clock to 1 o'clock position, 20–30 cm rod tip movement, with a smooth, gentle action that just makes the lure rattle. **Step 4:** Slowly drop the rod back to the 2 o'clock position retrieving line as you do so. Then, keeping a tight line (this is very important) allow the lure to settle back to the bottom. **Step 5:** As soon as the lure hits the bottom repeat the process.

These detailed diagrams of the lure during the retrieve show that the passive retrieve imitates a small fish fossicking or shuffling on the bottom. The aggressive retrieve is more representative of an injured baitfish.

Passive retrieve lure path.

TOP FRESHWATER TECHNIQUES

ECHNIQUE 10

ggressive retrieve

he aim of this retrieve is to simulate a wounded juvenile fish.

tep 1: Cast and allow the lure to sink to the bottom.

tep 2: As soon as the lure has hit the bottom start to retrieve.

tep 3: Lift the rod from a 3 o'clock to a 1 o'clock position with a subtle sharp lift of 50–60 cm rod tip novement. This will quickly jerk the lure off the bottom and give it a good rattle in doing so. The sharp attle of these lures can often be heard when the lure is 5 or 6 metres below the boat!

tep 4: Slowly drop the rod back to the 3 o'clock position while retrieving line. Then, keeping a tight ne (this is very important), allow the lure to settle back to the bottom.

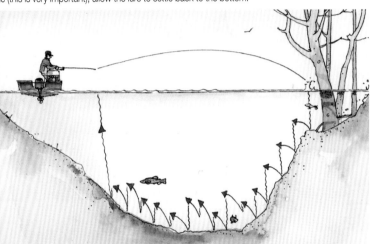

Here the retrieve pattern is illustrated while working the old river bed.
For aggressive fish use larger and occasional double 'agitator' hops.
With passive fish, work the bottom.

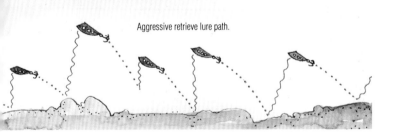

Aggressive retrieve lure path.

LEARN HOW TO CATCH MORE FISH

From the team at: